THE HORSE RACING PLACE BET INVESTMENT STRATEGY

EX BOOKIE TURNED PUNTER
GUIDE ON HOW TO BEAT
THE BOOKMAKERS AT
THEIR OWN GAME

BY TIM RUSSELL

CONTENTS

Place Betting Method Operation 04

Note All Bets Are In The Place Market Only 11

Result I 12

Result II 15

Class Pars 22

Types Of Races to Avoid 24

Staking Selection 25

Betting Banks 26

Summary Of Selection Method 34

PLACE BETTING METHOD OPERATION

There is nothing more frustrating as a punter than to spend hours going through the form book each morning and betting on the horses you select only to see them getting beat into second place. There are lots of factors in a race which determine the outcome but when you think you are on the best horse in the race and you see it lose because the jockey has given it a bad ride or the horse made a blunder at the last or got squeezed for room on the run in etc. etc. is very frustrating and hard to take, especially when runs like these seem to happen for long peiods of time. I am not a sore loser and only expect around 30% of the horses I select to win anyway (2 out of three lose) with the selection stragey I used, and if the prices are right then you will make money in the long term with such a strike rate, but a recent spate of seconditis made me rethink my whole selection strategy and the way I bet on horses.

At a recent planned visit to my local track meant I had done my homework on the races beforehand regarding form analysis of the six races on the card that day. The horses I fancied finished second in four races and third in the other two none were each way prices, though I have never struck an each way bet in my life, but I thought on this day I would take a different approach and back the horses on course using my mobile phone on my betfair account and back them in the place market only, I also did a placepot on the tote on the six selections to add more a little more spice to the mix.

My first selection finished second at 1.32, my second selection finished third at 1.45, my third selection finished second at 1.12, my fourth selection finished third at 1.64, my fith selection finished second at 1.3 and my last selection finished second again at 1.38

If I had been backing the selections win only I would have had a very frustrating day as two of the selections that finished second were beaten in very close photo finishes and as previously mentioned one of the runners was given far too much to do and the other one would have won apart form a bad error and swerving on the run in, but hey ho, Such is life!! And my run of seconds continued!! So the decision to bet place only was a wise move. I had uppped my stakes from my usual £50 per race when I do go to the course to £100 to take into account I was betting place only and my risk of getting a return on the races had been reduced in doing so. The combined odds that day were 1.32, 1.45, 1.12, 1.64 and 1.38 less the 5% betfair Commision my clear profit on the day was £181 for a £600 outlay, a 30% return on my money on the day which was fair enough for me, I also had the placepot up which again I did to £50 and that returned me £475 which was a bit of a bonus as doing that was a bit of an afterthought which paid off, but of course the placepot scenario has nothing to do with this strategy but the 6 placed horses have.

When I returned home that evening I was quite excited about the fact I had changed my betting strategy on the day and the fact I had done so made the difference between me walking away £600 down, to being £181 in profit that's quite a diference, of course it would have only taken one of the placed horses to finish out of the frame and the days balance sheet would not have looked so good.

If I was to continue place betting I now I had to spend a bit of time looking for a solid strategy that could see me turn the idea of backing for a place only into a profitable venture. The first thing I had to do was change my mindset, as I have stated I had never placed an each way bet in my life, I once read an article called each way betting is for whimps and have always gone along with that strain of thought, I had always backed plenty of winners and that is how I made money from betting on the horses. My strategy would be not to look any further than the first three in the betting and take a good look at their form to see if I thought their market position was justified. If I could make a case for any horse on the day I would back them to win and this has served me well up to having this spate of seconditis, was it sheer bad luck, poor selection process? Or a Lack of confidence? Or a lttle of all three? I really don't know what it was but I wasn't finding enough winners to keep my betting bank in the black. If this happens then its back to the drawing board for me and that's exactly what I decided to do.

As a serious punter I have always spent money on form books, I have never been able to quite understand the fact that at the course or in the bookmakers you see punters with bits of paper with selections written on them or cut outs from a daily tabloid paper to use for their selections, its not difficult to see why the bookmakers win at this game!! If you are going to follow this strategy and use the same methodology I do, then unfortunately you are going to have to spend money on form too to find the selections. (more of this later)

In the past I have used a variety of form books, my first serious bit of form was weekender newspaper, I then moved on to subscribing to a now defunct weekly updated form book called superform. The form pages came through the post and were updated on a weekly basis which unfortunatley meant if a horse was turned out quickly you could not keep tabs on the form, so an express version was introduced and the form was updated twice a week, it then went online which was great. Superform ratings were the best I have ever used. I still miss those ratings as the priod I did use their form I was backing some big priced winners that were top rated and actually making the game pay big time, I did actually go through a phase where my bets were restricted both online and in my local bookmakers, nice to see them quake!! that's when you know you are doing something right on a regualr basis.

I have also used Timeform and to this day use the Racing Post both paper versions and online. The problem with the aforementioned is that runners that are clear in their ratings generally end up short priced favourites and over bet by the mainstream punters, whereas using an undersubcribed form book such as Superform may give you an edge. Unfortunately now we all sing from the same songsheet as the Racing Post is the only daily racing paper available and the only one hanging on the bookmakers walls so highlighted good things by the Racing Post ratings or tipsters should really be considered lay material as they are definitely over bet.

More recently to get an edge I have been looking at speed ratings, I do think this is an area in racing form that is overlooked by punters and an invaluable tool now especially so with the introduction of all weather racing, these tracks seem to be in the ascendence and possibly the future of flat racing in this country? Many people still berate these tracks and the low grade racing that takes place on them, but the quality of racing is improving and its becoming an area of racing I am taking a very keen interest in. This takes me on to the form book I use for these selections. I came across a site that produces speed ratings at www.informracing.com and thought I would give their information and ratings a try, I assume the site does not have a huge subscription base so their ratings may be underutilised so thought I would test their ratings over a period to see how I went on with them and whether or not they could be used in my place betting strategy. The answer to that question was yes. I think at present Inform ratings cost £35 per month for subscriptions to their site, they offer a discount if you sign up for the year which is a fee of £120 so a huge saving there. I suggest you sign up for the first month and see how you go using this system and their ratings to test whether the method truly works for you.

The best way of signing up for these is to use the link in the homepage of www.bettingsystem.info or simply click on the SPEED RATINGS TAB on their homepage, by going through this site you can often get the latest discounts being offered by the vendor.

Having Signed up to Inform Racing which is a wise move anyway as I am sure you will use their ratings to great effect using this method or infact other strategies from their site. They also have a great tool on there which may be helpful to you in their system builder, definitely worth taking a look at. Anyway enough about form now and on with the process of finding selections. What I like about Inform ratings is that they can be accessed the night before racing takes place, which means you can have your selections sorted out the night before racing commences the following day, place your bets and get that chore out of the way. It will really only take you minutes to find your selections as the inform site is very easy to navigate through as all of the races are on one page When you have subscribed to their ratings go to their homepage at www.informracing.com

Go to their meetings page which will bring up the following:-

7

THE HORSE RACING PLACE BET INVESTMENT STRATEGY

Todays racing was taking place on the 7/3/2019

📅 Today

CARLISLE

CHELMSFORD (A.W)

SOUTHWELL (A.W)

WINCANTON

When you go into their site you will see that there is a list of courses where todays racing is taking place, today we have reading from the top down a jumps meeting at Carlisle, an AW flat meeting at Chelmsford, an AW flat meeting at Southwell and finally another jumps meeting at Wincanton

Click on the top meeting and work your way through the card and repeat this process until you have gone through the whole of the days racing What we are looking for is the following to arrive at a selection:-

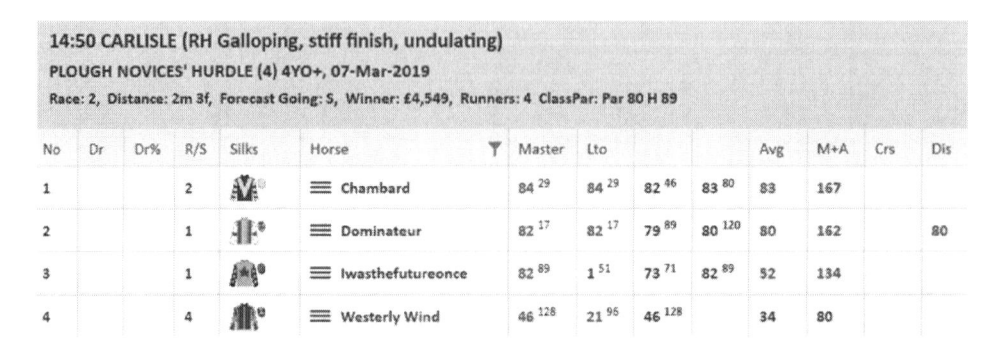

14:50 CARLISLE (RH Galloping, stiff finish, undulating)
PLOUGH NOVICES' HURDLE (4) 4YO+, 07-Mar-2019
Race: 2, Distance: 2m 3f, Forecast Going: S, Winner: £4,549, Runners: 4 ClassPar: Par 80 H 89

No	Dr	Dr%	R/S	Silks	Horse	Master	Lto			Avg	M+A	Crs	Dis
1			2		Chambard	84 ^{29}	84 ^{29}	82 ^{46}	83 ^{80}	83	167		
2			1		Dominateur	82 ^{17}	82 ^{17}	79 ^{89}	80 ^{120}	80	162		80
3			1		Iwasthefutureonce	82 ^{89}	1 ^{51}	73 ^{71}	82 ^{89}	52	134		
4			4		Westerly Wind	46 ^{128}	21 ^{96}	46 ^{128}		34	80		

In the 14.50 Race at Carlisle we note the ratings on the Inform site. Chambard is **CLEAR top rated 84** in this race in both the **MASTER RATING COLUMN** and the **Lto Column** this means that this horse is a possible selection for us today note that both ratings must be the same e.g. 84 Master – 84 Lto **if there is a discrepancy in the figures then no bet**

9 U 2 1 2   Chambard

The horse must have been placed either 1st, 2nd or 3rd on its last outing in the CURRENT season Chambard has form figures of 9U212 so finished second on its last run

Since a win: 46 days - 1 runs
Won right handed: 1/2 (50%)   Days since last run: 29
                                Days off before a win: 34
OR Today: HDL 125 (+0)

You can see that the possible selection Chambard had his last run 29 days ago which means that the form is current, note that this information is found by hovering your mouse over Chambard on the Inform site, this brings a up a box with the horses lifetime data and statistics

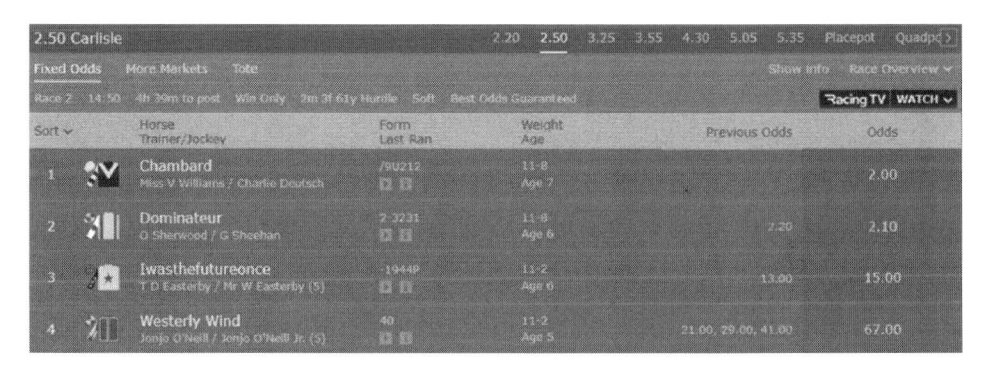

	Horse Trainer/Jockey	Form Last Ran	Weight Age	Previous Odds	Odds
1	Chambard Miss V Williams / Charlie Deutsch	/9U212	11-8 Age 7		2.00
2	Dominateur O Sherwood / G Sheehan	2-3231	11-8 Age 6	2.20	2.10
3	Iwasthefutureonce T D Easterby / Mr W Easterby (5)	-1944P	11-2 Age 6	13.00	15.00
4	Westerly Wind Jonjo O'Neill / Jonjo O'Neill Jr. (5)	40	11-2 Age 5	21.00, 29.00, 41.00	67.00

Our next step is to see where the horse is positioned in the betting market. I generally look at this information the night before racing or between 8.30am the day of racing, the time you look at this should really be before 9.30am as the markets tend to change after that time of the day when the money starts to come from the wider betting public. This aside, Chambard is the bookies overnight favourite on the site where I check the odds, so their odds compilers think it has the best chance in the race, note that the site I use who are quick to price up the following days racing is www.bet365.com I do actually have an account with this site but that is not necessary to get this information

Chambard qualifies as a selection as it fits the simple criteria I look for

1-   **TOP RATED IN THE MASTER and LTO COLUMNS ON THE INFORM RACING SITE.**

2-   **HAS PLACED FORM IN THE CURRENT SEASON 1st, 2nd or 3rd**

3-   **IS FAVOURITE ON THE WWW.BET365.COM BOOKMAKERS SITE BEFORE 9.30am**

The method is a simple as that so therefore as a bet the only thing left for you to do is to place your bet on the selection, to do this I use the biggest betting exchange to place my bets but there is no need to use this site as most bookmakers take place only bets. The reason I use them is that I think overall you do get slightly better odds if using betfair SP even after their 5% commission is taken off the price, I also like to use different bookmakers for different strategies and betfair is the site I have chosen to use for this particular strategy

THE HORSE RACING PLACE BET INVESTMENT STRATEGY

NOTE ALL BETS ARE IN THE PLACE MARKET ONLY

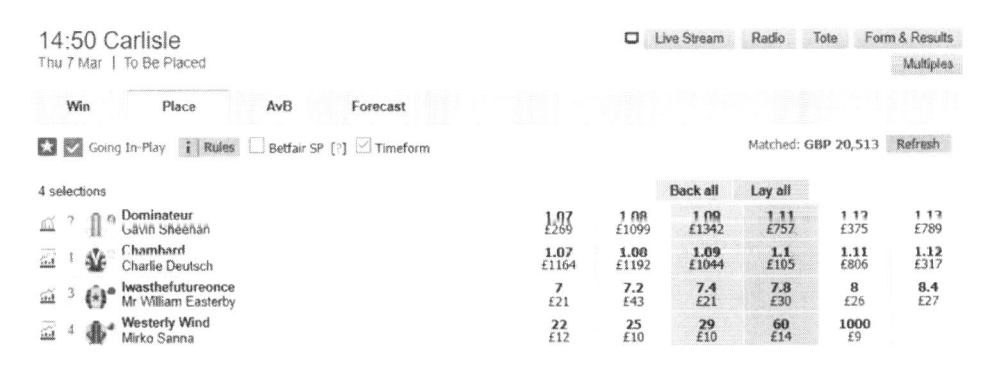

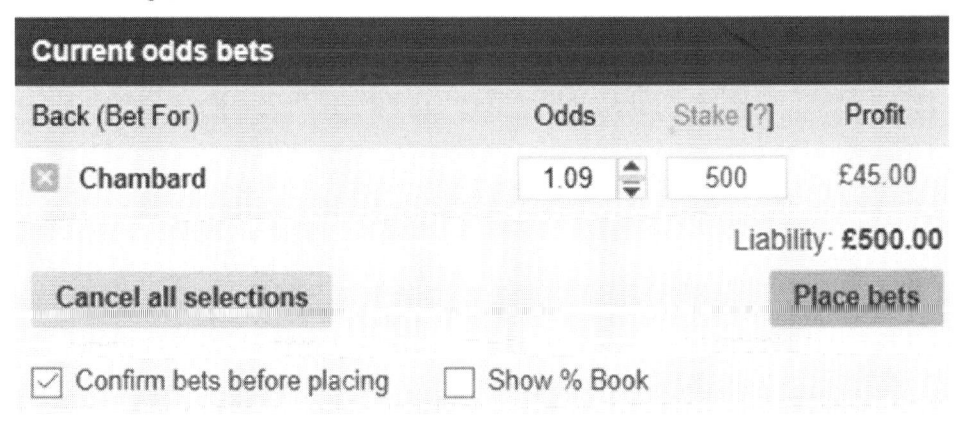

This selection is very skinny in the market at only 1.09 and shares this position with Dominatuer note that there are only four runners and this does look a two horse race on form, my £500 stake will currently return me £45 but I back selections to Betfair SP so I don't know until the race is in progress what price I have actually got until the race is off.

THE HORSE RACING PLACE BET INVESTMENT STRATEGY

RESULT I

Pos	Btn	Horse Name / Pedigree	TFR	Tflg	Jockey / Trainer	Age (Equip)	Wgt (OR)	ISP	BSP (Place)	Hi/Lo
1	0	2. DOMINATEUR (FR)	<		Gavin Sheehan / Oliver Sherwood	6	11-8	8/13f	1.67 (1.11)	1.75/-
		Subscribe to see the Premium Race Report for DOMINATEUR (FR) in this race								
2	1	1. CHAMBARD (FR)	<		Charlie Deutsch / Venetia Williams	7	11-8	13/8	2.86 (1.16)	-/2.58

The top two in the market actually fought out the finish with a big gap back to the third and fourth horses, we were never going to get a good price for this selection but did beat the price when I actually placed the bet by leaving it to run at betfair SP

15:55 CARLISLE (RH Galloping, stiff finish, undulating)
WATCH RACING TV NOW NOVICES' HANDICAP HURDLE (0-100) (5) 4YO+, 07-Mar-2019
Race: 4, Distance: 2m 1f, Forecast Going: S, Winner: £4,159, Runners: 8 ClassPar: Par 77 H 80

No	Dr	Dr%	R/S	Silks	Horse	Master	Lto			Avg	M+A	Crs	Dis
1			4		Emissaire	69 ^{51}	69 ^{51}	28 ^{81}	66 ^{98}	54	123	28	
2			4		Captain Kurt	79 ^{68}	79 ^{68}	47 ^{106}	53 ^{131}	60	139		
3			2		Rafferty	61 ^{156}	51 ^{41}	47 ^{69}	39 ^{96}	46	107		61
4			2		Pads	73 ^{11}	73 ^{11}	68 ^{58}	61 ^{84}	67	140	73	
5			2		Christmas In Usa	87 ^{10}	87 ^{10}	69 ^{84}	58 ^{118}	71	158		
6			4		Infiniti	42 ^{125}	40 ^{56}	35 ^{83}	42 ^{125}	39	81		35
7			4		Byronegetonefree		47 *	60 *	47 *	51	51		
8			2		Cyrano Star	64 ^{214}	1 ^{10}	45 ^{16}	59 ^{39}	35	99		59

In the 15.55 Race at Carlisle we have another possible selection note the ratings on the Inform ratings site. Christmas In Usa is **clear top rated 87** in this race in both the **MASTER RATING COLUMN** and the **Lto Column** this means that this horse is a possible selection for us today

5 7 5 F P 4 0 / 6 P 6 4 4 2 6 F - 6 4 1   Christmas In Usa

Since a win: 10 days - 0 runs
Days since last run: 10
Days off before a win: 74

The horses last time out position was a win and that win was achieved 10 days ago so the form is current

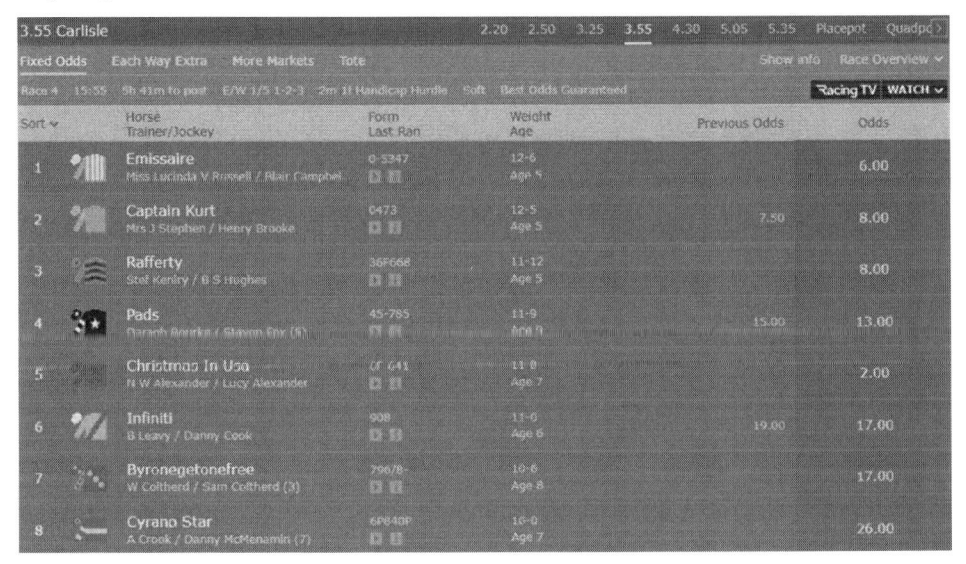

The horse is quoted 2.00 on the bet365 betting site and is favourite so therefore qualifies as a selection

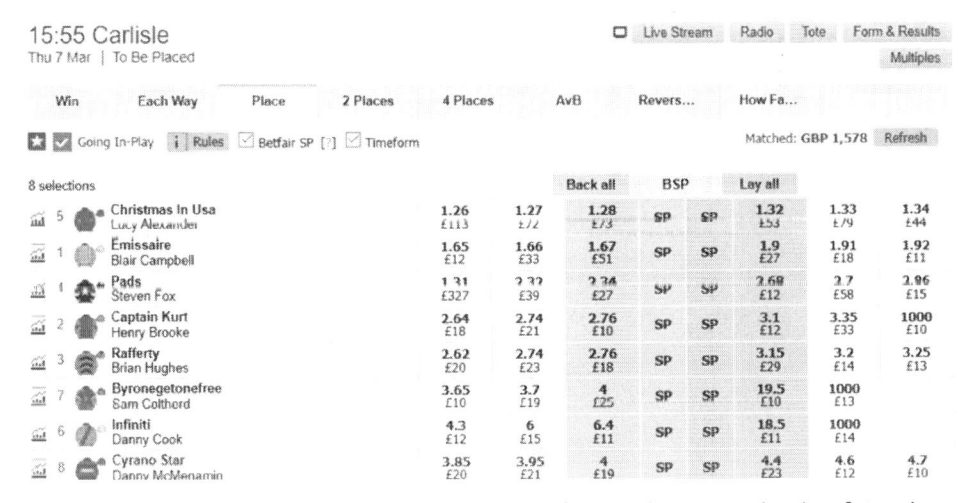

The horse is presently priced up at 1.28 for a place on the betfair place market

THE HORSE RACING PLACE BET INVESTMENT STRATEGY

3 to be placed

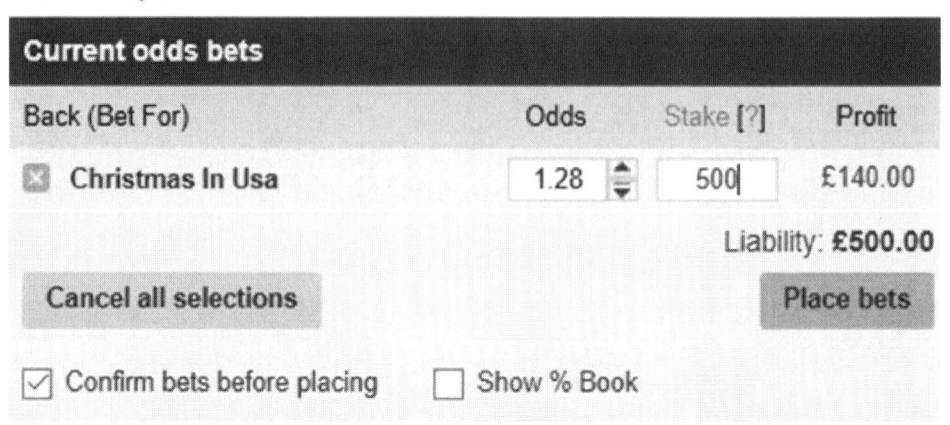

Current odds bets			
Back (Bet For)	Odds	Stake [?]	Profit
☒ Christmas In Usa	1.28	500	£140.00

Liability: **£500.00**

Cancel all selections Place bets

☑ Confirm bets before placing ☐ Show % Book

I have placed my bet at betfair SP the potential return at present is £140

RESULT II

Pos	Btn	Horse Name / Pedigree	TFR	Tfig	Jockey / Trainer	Age (Equip)	Wgt (OR)	ISP	BSP (Place)	Hi/Lo
1		5. CHRISTMAS IN USA (FR)	<		Lucy Alexander / N. W. Alexander	7 (v+t)	11-8 (90)	6/5f	2.25 (1.35)	29/-
2	2½	8. CYRANO STAR (FR)	<		Danny McMenamin (7) / Andrew Crook	7 (s)	10-0 (68)	14/1	18.19 (4.06)	-/1.1
3	16	2. CAPTAIN KURT	<		Henry Brooke / Jackie Stephen	5	12-5 (101)	6/1	7.88 (2.2)	-/3.2

Our selection won the race as I expected though the 2nd gave it a run and looked like the possible winner until a blunder at the last allowing our selection to go on and win, there was a massive gap back to the third horse so the selection was a solid one again

15:15 WINCANTON (RH Galloping)
ALL SPORT INSURANCE MARES' NOVICES' HURDLE (4) 4YO+, 07-Mar-2019
Race: 4, Distance: 1m 7f, Forecast Going: GS, Winner: £4,224, Runners: 12 ClassPar: Par 77 H 92

No	Dr	Dr%	R/S	Silks	Horse	Master	Lto			Avg	M+A	Crs	Dis
1			2		Ask Jilly	52 ^{65}	52 ^{65}	24 ^{88}	1 ^{124}	26	78		
2			4		Dieu Benisse	1 ^{38}	1 ^{38}	1 ^{71}		1	2	1	1
3			4		I'm A Believer	66 ^{55}	54 ^{15}	66 ^{55}		60	126		
4			1		Illuminated Beauty	67 ^{14}	67 ^{14}			67	134		
5					Leave My Alone								
6					Loquacious Lady								
7			1		Penny Pool	84 ^{71}	36 ^{17}	84 ^{71}		60	124	84	84
8			1		Perfect Myth	74 ^{303}	72 ^{18}	71 ^{79}	55 ^{275}	66	140		
9			4		Saumur	73 ^{51}	73 ^{51}			73	146		
10			1		Sweet Adare	82 ^{16}	82 ^{16}	44 ^{113}	72 ^{130}	66	148		
11			4		Westerner Ocean	50 ^{31}	37 ^{19}	50 ^{31}		44	94	37	37
12			2		Miranda	84 ^{29}	84 ^{29}			84	168		

In the 15.15 Race at Wincanton we note the ratings on the Inform site, Miranda is **clear top rated 84** in this race in both the **MASTER RATING COLUMN** and the **Lto Column** this means that this horse is a possible selection for us today

THE HORSE RACING PLACE BET INVESTMENT STRATEGY

1 Miranda

Since a win: 29 days - 0 runs

Won right handed: 1/1 (100%)   Days since last run: 29

Days off before a win:

The possible selection has only run the once to date and that was 29 days ago in a race it won so the form is current

Sort	Horse Trainer/Jockey	Form Last Ran	Weight Age	Previous Odds	Odds
1	Ask Jilly / M R Bosley / Kielan Woods	000	11-0 Age 6	201.00, 151.00	201.00
3	I'm A Believer / A King / Wayne Hutchinson	49	11-0 Age 5	17.00, 17.00, 21.00, 34.00	67.00
4	Illuminated Beauty / K C Bailey / David Bass	P-217	11-0 Age 6	21.00, 21.00, 26.00, 29.00	34.00
5	Leave My Alone / Mrs R Ford / R P McLernon	7F1	11-0 Age 6	26.00, 21.00, 34.00, 51.00	67.00
6	Loquacious Lady / H Fry / Kieron Edgar (3)	1	11-0 Age 5	15.00, 17.00, 26.00, 29.00	51.00
7	Penny Poet / N P Mulholland / N D Fehily	27	11-0 Age 6	9.00, 11.00, 17.00, 19.00	21.00
8	Perfect Myth / H Whittington / Harry Bannister	3-5034	11-0 Age 5	13.00, 11.00, 12.00, 15.00	17.00
9	Saumur / D J Coakley / J J Burke	4	11-0 Age 7	7.00, 6.50, 7.00, 9.00	11.00
10	Sweet Adare / V R A Dartnall / James Best	41-782	11-0 Age 6	7.00, 6.00	5.50
11	Westerner Ocean / A Dunn / M G Nolan	2/5-78	11-0 Age 7	101.00, 81.00, 151.00	201.00
12	Miranda / P F Nicholls / H Cobden	1	10-12 Age 4	2.37, 1.40, 1.36, 1.40	1.36

The horse is quoted a very short priced favourite on the bet 365 website so therefore qualifies as a selection

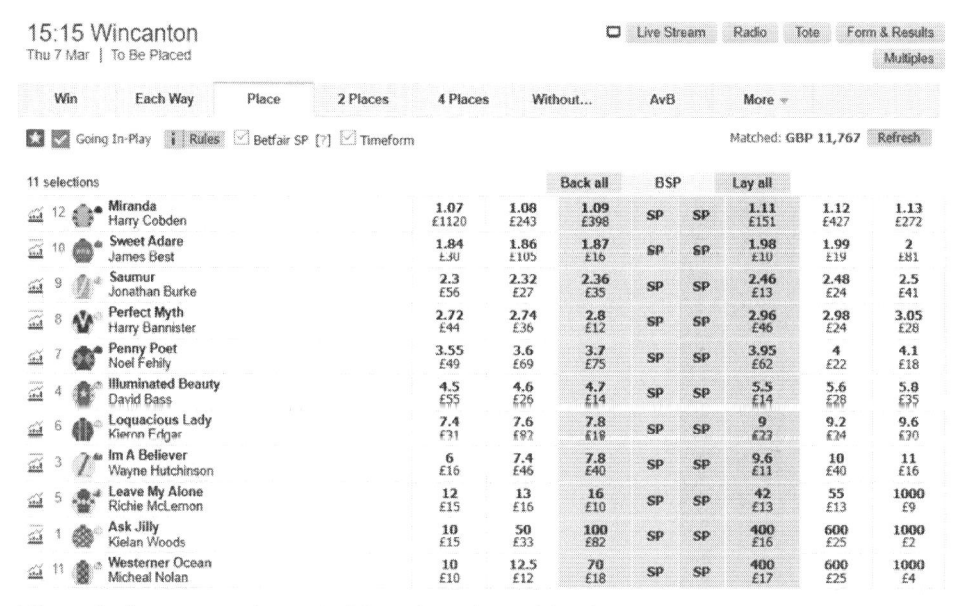

THE HORSE RACING PLACE BET INVESTMENT STRATEGY

Miranda is a very short 1.09 to be placed in the race

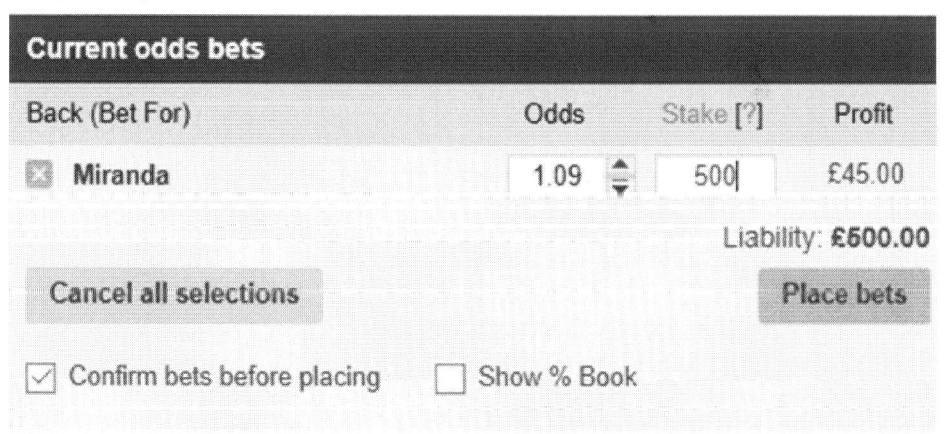

3 to be placed

My bet is placed with a potential return of £45 but again as the bet is placed to BFSP I don't actually know what my return will be until the race is off

17

THE HORSE RACING PLACE BET INVESTMENT STRATEGY

Pos	Stn	Horse Name / Pedigree	TFR	Tflg	Jockey / Trainer	Age (Equip)	Wgt (OR)	ISP	BSP (Place)	Hi/Lo
1		12. MIRANDA (IRE)	<		Harry Cobden / Paul Nicholls	4	10-12	2/5f	1.48 (1.11)	1.5/-
		Subscribe to see the Premium Race Report for MIRANDA (IRE) in this race								
2	3	10. SWEET ADARE (IRE)	<		James Best / Victor Dartnall	6	11-0 (t)	4/1	7.71 (1.66)	/6.2
		Subscribe to see the Premium Race Report for SWEET ADARE (IRE) in this race								
3	3½	8. PERFECT MYTH	<		Harry Bannister / Harry Whittington	5	11-0	8/1	15.04 (2.29)	/9.6

The selection cruised into the race and simply outclassed her rivals so again was in no danger of not getting into the frame

15:45 WINCANTON (RH Galloping)
FOLLOW US ON TWITTER @STARSPORTS_BET MAIDEN HURDLE (DIV I) (5) 4YO+, 07-Mar-2019
Race: 5, Distance: 2m 4f, Forecast Going: GS, Winner: £3,249, Runners: 11 ClassPar: Par 70 H 88

No	Dr	Dr%	R/S	Silks	Horse	Master	Lto			Avg	M+A	Crs	Dis
1			4		Avoir De Soins	1 [104]	1 [104]			1	2		
2			1		Banana Joe	63 [83]	63 [83]	40 [138]		52	115		
3			2		Dawn Sunrise	14 [12]	14 [12]			14	28		
4			2		Endless Flight	67 [65]	67 [65]	60 [89]	54 [348]	60	127		
5			1		Lord Duveen	67 [145]	58 [19]	67 [145]	59 [355]	61	128	58	
6			3		Palixandre	40 [288]	40 [288]			40	80		
7					Pres								
8			3		Storm Arising	77 [48]	77 [48]	72 [89]	66 [106]	72	149		
9			1		Talktomenow	81 [108]	63 [84]	81 [108]		72	153		
10			4		Vis A Vis	84 [17]	84 [17]			84	168		
11			4		West Chinnock		5 ˙			5	5		

In the 15.45 Race at Wincanton we note the ratings on the Inform site. Vis A Vis is clear top rated 84 in this race in both the MASTER RATING COLUMN and the Lto Column this means that this horse is a possible selection for us today

2   Vis A Vis

Since a win: 0 days - 1 runs
Days since last run: 17
Days off before a win:

The horse has only run the once where it finished 2nd and that was 17 days ago so the form is current

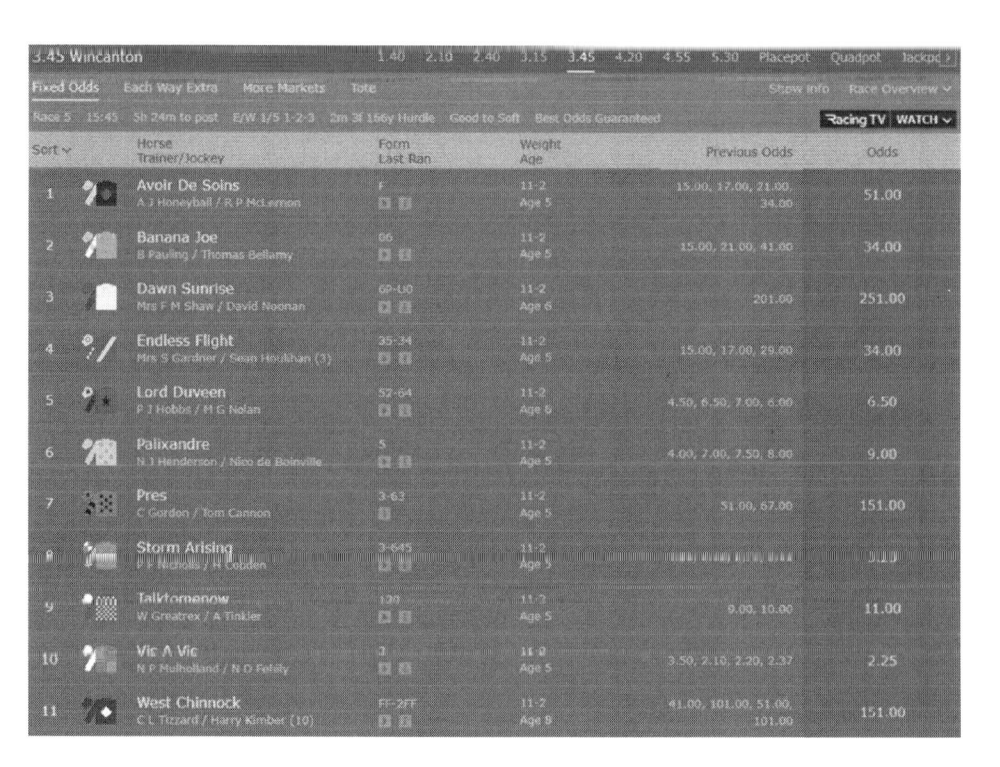

#	Horse / Trainer / Jockey	Form / Last Ran	Weight / Age	Previous Odds	Odds
1	Avoir De Soins / A J Honeyball / R P McLernon	F	11-2 Age 5	15.00, 17.00, 21.00, 34.00	51.00
2	Banana Joe / B Pauling / Thomas Bellamy	06	11-2 Age 5	15.00, 21.00, 41.00	34.00
3	Dawn Sunrise / Mrs F M Shaw / David Noonan	6P-U0	11-2 Age 6	201.00	251.00
4	Endless Flight / Mrs S Gardner / Sean Houlihan (3)	35-34	11-2 Age 5	15.00, 17.00, 29.00	34.00
5	Lord Duveen / P J Hobbs / M G Nolan	52-64	11-2 Age 6	4.50, 6.50, 7.00, 6.00	6.50
6	Palixandre / N J Henderson / Nico de Boinville	5	11-2 Age 5	4.00, 7.00, 7.50, 8.00	9.00
7	Pres / C Gordon / Tom Cannon	3-63	11-2 Age 5	51.00, 67.00	151.00
8	Storm Arising / P F Nicholls / H Cobden	3-645	11-2 Age 5		
9	Talktomenow / W Greatrex / A Tinkler	139	11-2 Age 5	9.00, 10.00	11.00
10	Vis A Vis / N P Mulholland / N D Fehily	2	11-2 Age 5	3.50, 2.10, 2.20, 2.37	2.25
11	West Chinnock / C L Tizzard / Harry Kimber (10)	FF-2FF	11-2 Age 9	41.00, 101.00, 51.00, 101.00	151.00

THE HORSE RACING PLACE BET INVESTMENT STRATEGY

The horse is quoted clear favourite on the bet365 website

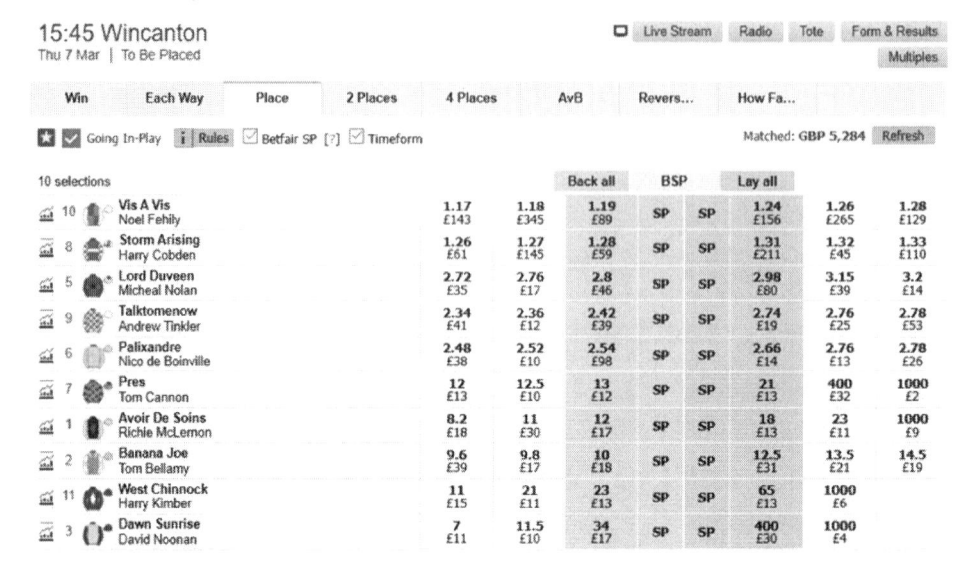

		Back all		BSP		Lay all		
10 Vis A Vis Noel Fehily	1.17 £143	1.18 £345	1.19 £89	SP	SP	1.24 £156	1.26 £265	1.28 £129
8 Storm Arising Harry Cobden	1.26 £61	1.27 £145	1.28 £59	SP	SP	1.31 £211	1.32 £45	1.33 £110
5 Lord Duveen Micheal Nolan	2.72 £35	2.76 £17	2.8 £46	SP	SP	2.98 £80	3.15 £39	3.2 £14
9 Talktomenow Andrew Tinkler	2.34 £41	2.36 £12	2.42 £39	SP	SP	2.74 £19	2.76 £25	2.78 £53
6 Palixandre Nico de Boinville	2.48 £38	2.52 £10	2.54 £98	SP	SP	2.66 £14	2.76 £13	2.78 £26
7 Pres Tom Cannon	12 £13	12.5 £10	13 £12	SP	SP	21 £13	400 £32	1000 £2
1 Avoir De Soins Richie McLernon	8.2 £18	11 £30	12 £17	SP	SP	18 £13	23 £11	1000 £9
2 Banana Joe Tom Bellamy	9.6 £39	9.8 £17	10 £18	SP	SP	12.5 £31	13.5 £21	14.5 £19
11 West Chinnock Harry Kimber	11 £15	21 £11	23 £13	SP	SP	65 £13	1000 £6	
3 Dawn Sunrise David Noonan	7 £11	11.5 £10	34 £17	SP	SP	400 £30	1000 £4	

3 to be placed

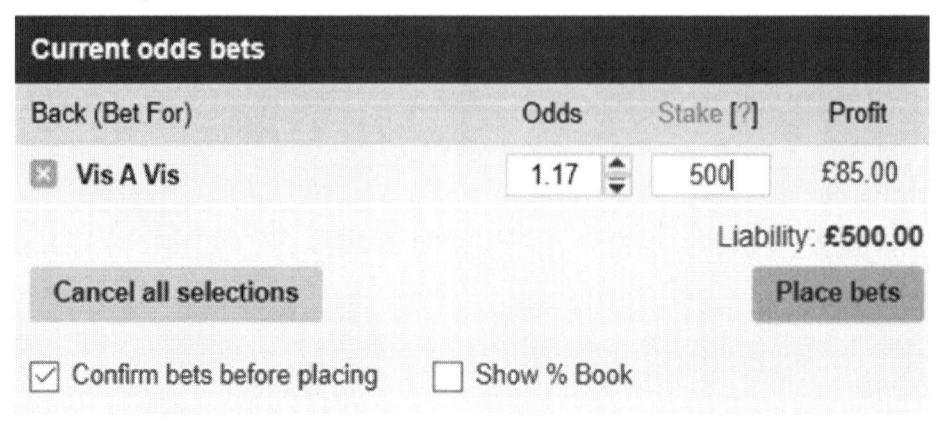

Current odds bets

Back (Bet For)	Odds	Stake [?]	Profit
Vis A Vis	1.17	500	£85.00

Liability: **£500.00**

Cancel all selections   Place bets

☑ Confirm bets before placing   ☐ Show % Book

Again we are looking at very skinny odds for the place, the race does look a two runner affair on paper

Pos	Btn	Horse Name / Pedigree	TFR	Tfig	Jockey / Trainer	Age (Equip)	Wgt (OR)	ISP	BSP (Place)	Hi/Lo
1		8. STORM ARISING (IRE)			Harry Cobden / Paul Nicholls	5	11-2	11/8jf	2.51 (1.2)	4/-
2	6	10. VIS A VIS			Noel Fehily / Neil Mulholland	5	11-2	11/8jf	2.53 (1.22)	-/1.44
3	26	5. LORD DUVEEN (IRE)			Micheal Nolan / Philip Hobbs	6	11-2	9/1	14 (2.47)	-/4.9

The results was as expected our selection fought out the finish with the horse I thought was the danger and the market got this spot on as they were sent off joint favourites, again there was a massive gap back to the third horse in the race

THE HORSE RACING PLACE BET INVESTMENT STRATEGY

CLASS PARS

Another part of the ratings site you need to pay very close attention to is the CLASS PARS

No	Dr	Dr%	R/S	Silks	Horse	Master				Avg	M+A	Crs	Dis
1		4			Emissaire	69 51	6 51	28 81	66 98	54	123	28	
2		4			Captain Kurt	79 68	9 68	47 106	53 131	60	139		
3		2			Rafferty	61 156	1 41	47 69	39 96	46	107		61
4		2			Pads	73 11	73 11	68 58	61 84	67	140	73	
5		2			Christmas In Usa	87 10	87 10	69 84	58 118	71	158		
6		4			Infiniti	42 125	40 56	35 83	42 125	39	81		35
7		4			Byronegetonefree		47 -	60 -	47 -	51	51		
8		2			Cyrano Star	64 214	1 10	45 16	59 39	35	99		59

15:55 CARLISLE (RH Galloping, stiff finish, undulating)
WATCH RACING TV NOW NOVICES' HANDICAP HURDLE (0-100) (5) 4YO+, 07-Mar-2019
Race: 4, Distance: 2m 1f, Forecast Going: S, Winner: £4,159, Runners: 8 ClassPar: Par 77 H 80

The Inform racing team post Class pars on their site, this figure represents the average speed figure produced by past winners of the race, noting this when looking for a selection should be advantageous, if our possible selection on the day has matched or bettered the speed par figure both in the Master column and the Lto (last time out) column then its ratings look reliable .If the horse was top rated in both columns yet falls below the par figure for the race, the race may be a weak affair and the form of the top rated selection not that strong and an upset may be likely. I do like to see a selection meet or better the par, all our selections today match or beat the speed par figure.

Note also that there is a figure alongside the Par in the case of the example shown H 80 this is the highest figure this race has produced and our possible selection beats this quite comfortably 87 both Master and Lto compared with a time of 80 for the highest winning time. This horse has shown form in its last race well up to winning this race quite comfortably and alongside placing a bet in my place method I will be having a separate win bet on this horse and do so whenever I come across a horse that beats the highest rating in both the Master and Lto columns. Doing so this week alone has produced four good winners at 11/4, 5/2, 2/1 and the above at 6/5 (an added bonus there for you to take note of)

TYPES OF RACES TO AVOID

There are races run in the racing calendar that I avoid like the plague!! These types of races throw up shock results and are best avoided

NATIONAL HUNT FLAT

These races are for national hunt bred horses but without the obstacles and the runners are generally unexposed types and winners who remain in this sphere have to carry penalties, I don't like betting in these races as generally the form cannot be relied upon

HUNTER CHASES

Unless you keep close tabs on the Point to Point action then you will not know an awful lot about the runners in this type of event, some of the professional yards have runners in these types of races but on the whole I find the form is difficult to assess and as there are only a few of these races run in a season they are best avoided

NOVICE / MAIDENS

There are many novice and maiden events run throughout the year where many of the runners are making their racecourse debut so the form of horses that have already run in these events may not be strong enough to see off a newcomer especially if this debutant is a well - bred type from a top yard. Be very wary backing in these types of races and the point I make about speed pars is very relevant here, horses that have seen the track need to have shown a good rating to be considered. I also like to have seen at least a third of the runners in these events to have seen the racetrack

STAKING SELECTIONS

This part of the method is just as important as the selection section for many reasons. Most punters fail to make it as they don't have the correct mindset and greed plays a massive factor in most punters make up. We all want to get rich quick but believe me this isn't going to happen with any method you choose to follow. If you like to back big priced winners then be prepared to encounter long losing runs that test your patience to the extreme. If you want lots of winners then you have to follow shorter priced selections and the odd loser or two can soon put you on the back foot. The game is not easy and I do believe that you have to take a different approach to most of the other people in the game to make it pay. I have tried everything and have some great selection methods in my armoury at present, the only time I lose is when I show signs of impatience or a lack of discipline which can happen to anyone from time to time. The successful punters are the ones who do not succumb to these urges and remain patient.

The perfect racing selection method has not yet been printed as it doesn't exist like I have stated the type of method or methods you choose to follow all have a downside and that is the unexpected losing runs. This is the time the ill disciplined punter will abandon their previously well thought out good intentions of sticking with the banking and staking strategy and chase losses or simply turn their back on the method completely and move on to the next latest greatest method for only the same scenario to occur over and over again. Does this ring a bell? Don't worry if it does, the cycle can be broken and you are not alone as I have been there many times in the past myself when things haven't worked out.

BETTING BANK

The key to making a success of your betting is to have a betting bank in place that will cover your expected losses and not to flinch when it comes close to doing so. The money you have set aside in the bank is money you have no other use for than to bet and possibly lose. I have blown betting banks in the past on ill thought out strategies or jumped in too quickly to use methods that have not been thoroughly tested, yes to get rich quick!! Firstly we need to examine the likely losing runs and to do this we need a good set of results to calculate this, I have published results from the 1st of January 2018 I could have gone back much further but there is no need. All of these results are up to date so a good 14 months, you would expect that everything that has occurred in this time period can be relied upon and can be considered reliable data but believe me nothing is set in stone when it comes to betting on horses, examine the table below:-

Losing run prediction tools

To help put things in perspective we can use prediction tools professional bettors use to estimate the likelihood of a losing run and its length in terms of bets.

First of all you need to work out the Median (average) odds of winners compared with the strike rate.

Then take a look at your betting bank and assess if you have enough money to cover the losing runs.

You can use the table below to calculate losing runs centred on strike rate. As you can see, the higher the strike rate is the lower sequence of consecutive losers is.

Strike Rate (%)	Maximum Losing Run
5	135
10	66
15	43
20	31
25	24
30	19
35	16
40	14
45	12
50	10
55	9
60	8
65	7
70	6
75	5
80	4
85	4
90	3
95	2

This method to date has produced **1904 bets in total (From 1/1/2018 to date) 1784 Placed (94% Strike Rate) +473.84 to BFSP**

If you examine the table we sit in between the 90 – 95% strike rate so can expect losing runs to occur up to three on the bounce and what I stated about, expect the unexpected to happen. After losing runs of only two, recently the method had a losing run of four which defies the above table but as I have been in racing for so long this does not surprise me and after encountering bank busting sequences using previous methods in the past that were obviously unexpected then I am afraid to say losing your bank must always be taken into consideration

Therefore the table above is a guide and must be used as such as it is a useful one to follow, what we must do is start with a bank that gets you over the longest losing run encountered, in this case you could say a 5 point bank would suffice, but that would not leave me sleeping easy on an evening, I have a bank double that size a bank of 10 points is where I started from. I therefore recommend you do the same, place a 10 point bank to one side and as stated a bank you can afford to lose.

Treat you betting like you would your own business, if necessary keep records of all of the bets you have struck, winning sequences, losing sequences, prices of winners and losers and of course all important profit and loss. If after a period a method shows less in the bank than when you initially started then its time to tweak the method or simply move on to something else. I genuinely hope this is not the case with this method. I do not stand still as a punter and if I spot something that I think may improve the current method I am using then I will implement this if I think it will improve the strike rate and profits.

Remember that when you walk into your high street bookies and see the plush carpets on the floor and their up to date furniture and bank of TV's, their staff kitted out in uniforms are paid to work in the shops who rush over to offer you free tea or coffee all day, its all paid for by the ill disciplined punters, you me and the rest. You can only beat them by playing them at their own game i.e. by being strict, following a method to the letter through good and bad times and keeping records of all of the bets you have struck in the past to see what you are doing right or where you are going wrong.

You may not believe this but bookmakers have losing runs too, I used to bet in a small independent bookmakers who had an office just down the street from where I lived and before I switched to betting online (which I am still not sure is a good thing) the guy who owned the shop, was a proper old style bookmaker told me that he had just encountered the worst two months he had known since he started in the business over 40 years ago. I asked if he was about to pack it in and he just laughed and replied no way. He stated he had enough in the bank to pay his staff and rent etc. and knew that things would return to normal shortly. He was right, the shops he owns are still in business and thriving. This is the mentality we must all take on board.

This method has had losing runs of one, two and four (only once) and winning runs that stretch into the nineties (once) seventies, sixties, fifties, with numerous runs of forties, thirties, twenties and lower these are the runs that offset the very low prices we are getting for only backing in the place markets. If backing selections to level stakes, the return on investment is pretty good with 474 points achieved from 1908 bets which is around 25% that makes the average price of winners around 1.25 (a quarter of your stake) this is because of the unbelievably long winning sequences, 90+ winners on the bounce to be honest is quite incredible

The method should be used as a long-term investment plan as profits are slowly ground out. One day you might win 1.5 points the next day lose 1.25 that's how it is, therefore consider using a staking plan to accelerate your profits and keep your interest in the method alive as methods that are slow to move the profits on can become boring, and there is a danger you may lose interest. I have included a record of a level staking plan and level stakes are eventually what you will have to place regardless of the staking plan you choose

I have stated that I use a 10 - point betting bank but this was used initially to build up my bank to a level where I am happy to revert back to level stakes, the plan works as follows. Your initial bank is 10 points you then divide this by 10 each time you place a bet so your first stake is 1 point (1/10th of the bank) if the horse wins say at 1.67 your bank would increase to 10.64 (5% commission taken off winnings if using betfair) so your next stake would be 1.06 if the horse had lost and your bank had dropped to 9 then your next stake would be 0.9

I have also shown how your bank would have faired using a 5% staking plan. This is obviously a slower less risky approach than the above but you still eventually reach a point where you would not get bets placed. Take a good look at the results tables and see which of the plans would suit your style of betting. When my bank reached £5000 I decided that was as far as I wanted to go so now bet £500 per race, if the bank goes above £5000 I take the profit, if it falls below I wait until I get back up to £5000 again before I take money out of the bank. Some weeks I may make 2-3 points profit x £500 is very good, I may have to go a week or two before I can take more profits but the method does make around a point profit per day.

WHAT ARE BETTING EXCHANGE PLACE MARKETS?

Place markets are as the name suggests, markets which let you bet on a selection for being 'placed'. E.g. a horse to finish 1st, 2nd or 3rd in a 8 runner or larger field. Now, the first and most essential thing to mention here is that these place markets are totally different to the popular Each Way (EW) betting markets offered by traditional bookmakers. The Each Way bet is actually 2 bets of equal stakes.

The 1st stake is on the selection to win and the 2nd is on it for being placed. So a £10 EW bet costs you £20 in total.

A £10 place bet on a Betting Exchange like Betfair is a single bet and therefore only costs you £10. If the selection finishes 1st, 2nd or 3rd, you collect your winnings and smile.

Consider it for a minute. How often have you been confident that a horse will be placed, but you have not been confident that it will win?

TRADITIONAL EACH WAY BETTING

Use the following example. A horse named 'I will be placed' which is available to back with traditional bookmakers at 4/1 (5.0). You are very confident that it can finish within the top 3 in a 12 runner field.

With a regular bookmaker, your **alternatives** are:

1. Take a risk on it winning and put a win single on it. E.g. £10 at 4/1

2. Place an Each Way bet on it. E.g. £10 EW at 4/1 (5.0). Total stakes £20. The bookies will pay you 1/5 odds on the place element of this E/W bet according to their standard EW rules. In our example which is the horse on the market to back at 5.0 this equates to 1.8

Now, the only result the above mentioned race will be profitable for you is if the horse actually wins. In the two cases you would get a nice profit if it wins. For option 1 you would win £40 profit and for option 2, £48 profit.

But, if as you suspected the horse only finishes in 2nd or 3rd place, you will lose money in both cases. With option 1 you obviously lose your entire stake so you are £10 down. With option 2, you win £8 on the Place side of the EW bet but still lose £2 overall as the win part of the bet would be a losing one.

ENTER THE BETTING EXCHANGE PLACE MARKETS

Using the above example and based on the odds of the other horses in the race, you would probably see the Betting Exchanges offering odds of around 1.60 - 2.00 (evens) on this horse being placed. You could therefore put your £10 place bet on around 1.8 and collect £8 profit (minus commission) assuming that the horse finishes 1st, 2nd or 3rd. Only if the horse finishes not in the top 3 you will lose your £10 stake.

We think this has got you thinking and you may probably understand the power in this straight away!

Along with a good staking plan and a sensible selection process, it can be typical to have very long winning streaks when backing horses being placed on the betting exchanges. These longer winning streaks more than compensate for the relatively short prices which are offered on selections to be placed.

A few essential points to keep in mind about place markets:

1. Unlike the betting exchange win markets, Place markets don't go "In-Running" once the race starts but this also applies to the traditional E/W bets offered by bookies.

2. If a race is planned as a 8 runner event or even more but several horses become non-runners leaving less than 8 runners, the betting exchanges still offer odds on 3 places. This is different to bookmakers who in these cases adjust their odds on the place payment from 1/5 to 1/4 of the win odds BUT they just pay out on 2 places. If a 5,6 or 7 runner field is shortened to fewer than 5 runners, the betting exchanges will still offer place markets and payout if the horse finishes 1st or 2nd.

The downside of the place markets on betfair is that there is not much liquidity about but I have always had my bets accepted when placing bets to betfair SP the other downside is of course when you are betting to skinny odds you still have to pay 5% commission, most bookmaker allow you to place bets in the place market only the size of your bets and high strike rate would come under scrutiny after a while with all high street / online bookmakers.

Consider using a betting bot if you cannot be around to place and adjust your stakes on each race, there are lots to chose from and all do 10% - 5% - Level stakes betting, another way of betting to say 10% is to adjust stakes after each days betting e.g. if your starting bank was 10 and the method throws up 4 selections on the day place a 1point bet on each selection, if the profit on the day was 2.5 then your bank moves up to 12.5 your stakes on your selection the next day would be 1.25 if the bets had all lost your bank would be 6 so your next stakes 0.6

I hope that I have covered all angles explaining this method to you. It's a very simple method to work out selections and staking but below is a quickfire summary of how to operate the method

A note of caution if you bet online. I used to be what I called a traditional bettor in the fact that all my bets were cash bets, I used to keep a stash of money at home and if I fancied a horse I would delve into the wad of cash and back the horse with my local bookmakers .If the horse won I would add to the stash until I eventually had to move some money into the bank. This method used to work well for me where i used to live as the staff in the shops were pretty discreet. I moved about 5 years ago and the new town I moved to had lots of bookmakers to go at, small independents and all of the big players Hills, Corals, Ladbrokes, Betfred all had multiple shops, as a winning punter who is a stranger too in a town you soon get noticed and I used to get fed up of the punters in the shops and staff asking for tips. They could also make life difficult when paying you out making you come back the following day etc, as they didn't have enough money in the shops. I got a bit stalled with all of this so decided to go online with all of my betting, it was more difficult for me to stay disciplined betting online as I was used to betting in cash, and its been a bit of a difficult transition for me. I do believe you have to move your discipline up a notch when the ability to place a bet is there at your fingertips either on your laptop or mobile.

SUMMARY OF SELECTION METHOD

1- Possible selections must be clear top rated in the **MASTER RATING** column and the Lto COLUMN both ratings must be equal E.g. MASTER 84 then Lto must be 84

2- The possible selection must be clear favourite in the early betting tissues up to 9.30am on the day of racing, prices can be checked from around 6.00pm the day before racing

3- Ratings must match or beat the par rating for that race

4- The possible selection must have been placed 1st, 2nd or 3rd in this the current season

4- Selections must be backed in the place markets only, either using betfair (to betfair SP) or with a traditional bookmaker such as bet365 who accept place only bets

5- Staking should be either level stakes, or 5% to 10% of the initial betting bank, note that other staking plans may work well but the above look to be the best options

I hope you enjoy using the method and that the results continue into the future.

All the best to you for now. Tim Russell

First 150 Bets at 10%

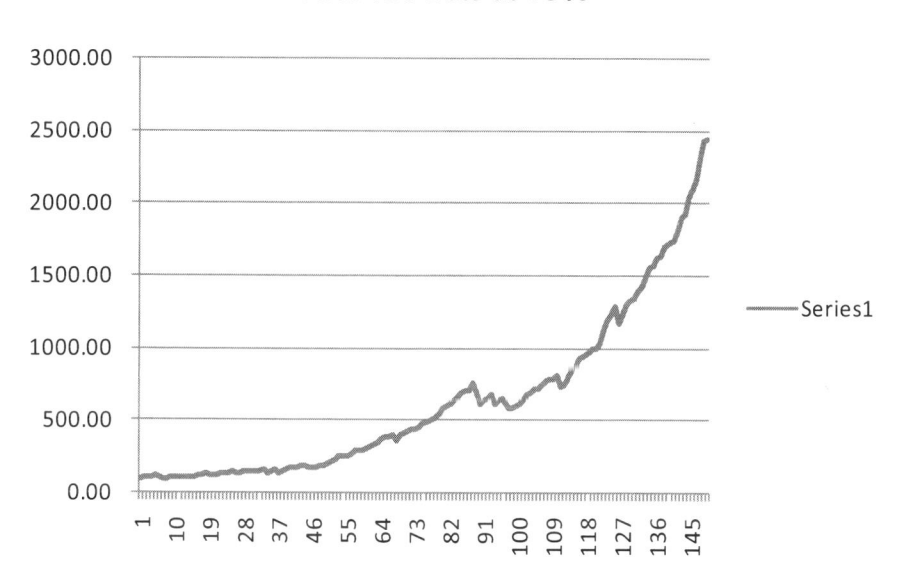

First 150 Bets at 5%

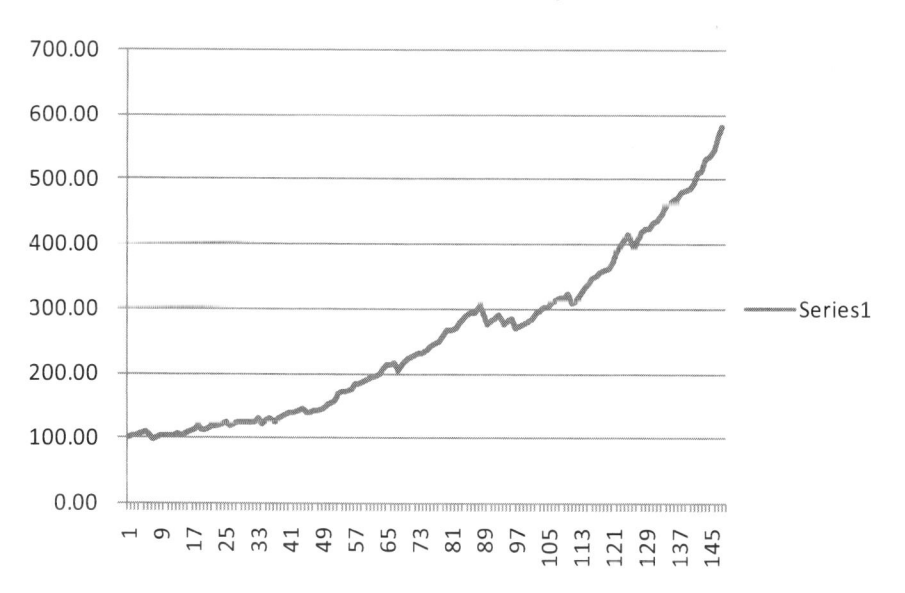

THE HORSE RACING PLACE BET INVESTMENT STRATEGY

1st January to 3rd February

				10% Stake			5% Stake		
Race Time	Course	Horse	Position	Place BSP	Place BSP	Profit	Bank Total	Stake 10%	Profit	Bank Total	Stake 5%

Race Time	Course	Horse	Position	Place BSP	Place BSP	Profit	Bank Total	Stake 10%	Profit	Bank Total	Stake 5%
01 Jan 2018 12:15	CHELTENHAM	Tikkanbar	1	1.64	0.61	6.10	100.00	10.00	3.05	100.00	5.00
01 Jan 2018 12:40	EXETER	Show On The Roa	1	1.16	0.76	1.61	106.10	10.61	0.82	103.05	5.15
01 Jan 2018 13:05	MUSSELBURGH	Cresswell Legend	1	1.63	1.36	6.45	107.71	10.77	3.27	103.87	5.19
01 Jan 2018 13:50	EXETER	Run To Milan	1	1.32	1.67	3.47	114.16	11.42	1.71	107.15	5.36
01 Jan 2018 15:05	FAKENHAM	Norse Light	0	0.00	0.67	-11.17	117.63	11.76	-5.44	108.86	5.44
01 Jan 2018 15:20	CATTERICK	Red Danaher	1	1.21	0.86	-10.65	106.45	10.65	-5.17	103.42	5.17
01 Jan 2018 15:40	FAKENHAM	Fresh New Dawn	2	1.64	1.47	5.83	95.81	9.58	3.14	98.25	4.91
02 Jan 2018 12:30	AYR	Blunder Buss	1	1.34	1.80	3.28	101.63	10.16	1.72	101.39	5.07
02 Jan 2018 13:35	AYR	Better Getalong	1	1.11	1.91	1.10	104.92	10.49	0.57	103.11	5.16
02 Jan 2018 18:40	NEWCASTLE (A.W)	Lord Of The Glen	1	1.24	2.13	2.42	106.01	10.60	1.24	103.68	5.18
03 Jan 2018 13:20	LUDLOW	Look My Way	1	1.10	2.22	1.03	108.43	10.84	0.52	104.93	5.25
03 Jan 2018 13:30	MUSSELBURGH	Mullaghmurphy	1	1.56	1.22	5.82	109.46	10.95	2.95	105.45	5.27
03 Jan 2018 15:10	SOUTHWELL (A.W)	Tatlisu	2	1.77	1.96	-11.53	115.28	11.53	-5.42	108.40	5.42
03 Jan 2018 15:20	LUDLOW	Hedgeinator	1	1.63	2.56	6.21	103.76	10.38	3.24	102.98	5.15
03 Jan 2018 17:10	WOLVERHAMPTON	Arnarson	1	1.90	3.41	9.40	109.97	11.00	4.78	106.23	5.31
04 Jan 2018 13:15	BANGOR-ON-DEE	Oneida Tribe	2	1.58	3.96	6.58	119.37	11.94	3.22	111.01	5.55
04 Jan 2018 14:05	NEWCASTLE (A.W)	Good Time Ahea	0	1.62	2.96	7.42	125.94	12.59	3.54	114.23	5.71
04 Jan 2018 14:40	NEWCASTLE (A.W)	Winds Of Fire	1	1.22	3.16	-13.34	133.36	13.34	-5.89	117.77	5.89
04 Jan 2018 15:10	NEWCASTLE (A.W)	Zabeel Star	1	1.33	3.47	3.76	120.03	12.00	1.85	111.88	5.59
04 Jan 2018 16:20	NEWCASTLE (A.W)	Ingleby Angel	3	1.35	3.81	4.12	123.79	12.38	1.99	113.72	5.69
04 Jan 2018 19:45	CHELMSFORD (A.W)	Udontdodou	1	1.56	4.33	6.80	127.91	12.79	3.24	115.72	5.79
05 Jan 2018 13:30	SOUTHWELL (A.W)	Heather Lark	3	1.25	4.57	3.20	134.71	13.47	1.49	118.96	5.95
05 Jan 2018 19:15	KEMPTON (A.W)	Night Of Glory	1	1.09	4.65	1.18	137.91	13.79	0.54	120.44	6.02
06 Jan 2018 12:05	LINGFIELD (A.W)	Zalshah	1	1.80	3.65	10.57	139.09	13.91	4.84	120.98	6.05
06 Jan 2018 12:40	LINGFIELD (A.W)	Craving	3	1.16	3.81	-14.97	149.66	14.97	-6.29	125.82	6.29
06 Jan 2018 15:55	CHEPSTOW	Good Boy Bobby	1	1.22	4.01	2.82	134.69	13.47	1.31	119.53	5.98
06 Jan 2018 20:45	KEMPTON (A.W)	Choice Encounte	1	1.48	4.47	6.27	137.51	13.75	2.90	120.85	6.04
08 Jan 2018 17:15	WOLVERHAMPTON	Cliffs Of Capri	2	1.10	4.57	1.37	143.78	14.38	0.62	123.75	6.19
08 Jan 2018 18:45	WOLVERHAMPTON	Victory Bond	1	1.17	4.73	2.34	145.14	14.51	1.06	124.37	6.22
09 Jan 2018 11:55	DONCASTER	Mount Mews	1	1.06	4.79	0.84	147.49	14.75	0.38	125.42	6.27
09 Jan 2018 12:25	DONCASTER	Black Op	1	1.07	4.85	0.99	148.33	14.83	0.44	125.80	6.29
09 Jan 2018 12:45	SOUTHWELL (A.W)	Lady Lintera	0	1.52	3.85	7.38	149.32	14.93	3.28	126.24	6.31
09 Jan 2018 12:55	DONCASTER	Tommy Rapper	1	1.15	4.00	-15.67	156.69	15.67	-6.48	129.52	6.48
10 Jan 2018 13:10	LINGFIELD (A.W)	Fortune And Glor	3	1.58	4.55	7.77	141.02	14.10	3.57	123.05	6.15
10 Jan 2018 14:50	LINGFIELD (A.W)	Make Music	0	1.62	3.55	8.76	148.79	14.88	3.93	126.61	6.33
10 Jan 2018 15:00	LUDLOW	Tb Broke Her	1	1.99	4.49	-15.76	157.56	15.76	-6.53	130.54	6.53
10 Jan 2018 15:25	LINGFIELD (A.W)	Something Lucky	1	1.95	5.39	12.80	141.80	14.18	5.89	124.01	6.20
10 Jan 2018 16:45	KEMPTON (A.W)	Albishr	2	1.69	6.05	10.13	154.60	15.46	4.48	129.90	6.50
10 Jan 2018 17:15	KEMPTON (A.W)	Sir Hamilton	1	1.33	6.37	5.16	164.73	16.47	2.22	134.38	6.72
11 Jan 2018 13:00	CATTERICK	Chu Chu Percy	1	1.46	6.80	7.42	169.90	16.99	3.14	136.60	6.83
11 Jan 2018 14:05	CATTERICK	Hear No Evil	1	1.11	6.90	1.85	177.32	17.73	0.77	139.74	6.99
11 Jan 2018 14:25	NEWCASTLE (A.W)	Esspeegee	1	1.30	7.19	5.11	179.18	17.92	2.11	140.51	7.03
11 Jan 2018 15:35	NEWCASTLE (A.W)	Battle Lines	0	1.54	6.19	9.45	184.28	18.43	3.85	142.62	7.13
11 Jan 2018 20:30	CHELMSFORD (A.W)	Mercury	2	1.34	6.51	-19.37	193.74	19.37	-7.32	146.47	7.32
12 Jan 2018 13:40	SEDGEFIELD	Quick Pick	1	1.10	6.60	1.66	174.36	17.44	0.70	139.15	6.96
12 Jan 2018 18:15	NEWCASTLE (A.W)	Wiff Waff	1	1.36	6.94	6.02	176.02	17.60	2.52	139.84	6.99
13 Jan 2018 12:15	LINGFIELD (A.W)	Every Chance	1	1.05	6.99	0.86	182.04	18.20	0.36	142.36	7.12
13 Jan 2018 13:00	KEMPTON	Secret Investor	2	1.30	7.28	5.21	182.90	18.29	2.14	142.72	7.14
13 Jan 2018 13:50	WARWICK	Duel At Dawn	1	1.78	8.02	13.94	188.12	18.81	5.65	144.86	7.24
13 Jan 2018 14:00	LINGFIELD (A.W)	Goring	1	1.38	8.38	7.29	202.05	20.21	2.86	150.51	7.53
13 Jan 2018 14:05	KEMPTON	Waiting Patiently	1	1.69	9.04	13.72	209.35	20.93	5.29	153.37	7.67
13 Jan 2018 15:25	WETHERBY	Newberry New	1	2.26	10.23	26.70	223.07	22.31	10.00	158.66	7.93
13 Jan 2018 15:55	WETHERBY	So Lonely	2	1.31	10.53	7.36	249.77	24.98	2.61	168.65	8.43
14 Jan 2018 12:40	KELSO	Coole Hall	1	1.10	10.62	2.44	257.13	25.71	0.86	171.27	8.56
14 Jan 2018 14:55	SOUTHWELL (A.W)	Snowy Winter	3	1.25	10.86	6.16	259.57	25.96	2.15	172.12	8.61
15 Jan 2018 17:10	WOLVERHAMPTON	Letmestopyouthe	1	1.99	11.80	24.99	265.74	26.57	8.63	174.27	8.71
16 Jan 2018 13:25	HEREFORD	Carole's Vigilante	1	1.09	11.88	2.49	290.73	29.07	0.82	182.90	9.15
16 Jan 2018 16:35	KEMPTON (A.W)	Olaudah	3	1.27	12.14	7.52	293.22	29.32	2.48	183.72	9.19
16 Jan 2018 18:40	KEMPTON (A.W)	Corinthia Knight	1	1.28	12.41	8.00	300.74	30.07	2.61	186.20	9.31
17 Jan 2018 15:10	MARKET RASEN	Iskabeg Lane	3	1.38	12.77	11.15	308.74	30.87	3.59	188.81	9.44
17 Jan 2018 15:20	LINGFIELD (A.W)	Spare Parts	1	1.41	13.15	12.46	319.88	31.99	3.94	192.40	9.62
17 Jan 2018 16:00	NEWCASTLE (A.W)	Apalis	1	1.32	13.45	10.10	332.34	33.23	3.14	196.34	9.82
17 Jan 2018 16:05	NEWBURY	Baddesley Knight	2	1.99	14.39	32.21	342.44	34.24	9.87	199.48	9.97
17 Jan 2018 16:30	NEWCASTLE (A.W)	Ingleby Angel	3	1.53	14.90	18.86	374.65	37.47	5.55	209.36	10.47
17 Jan 2018 17:30	NEWCASTLE (A.W)	Ode To Autumn	1	1.03	14.93	1.12	393.51	39.35	0.32	214.91	10.75
18 Jan 2018 12:40	LUDLOW	Melangerie	1	1.19	15.11	7.12	394.64	39.46	2.04	215.23	10.76
18 Jan 2018 13:10	WINCANTON	Tacenda	2	0.00	14.11	-38.17	401.76	40.18	-10.86	217.27	10.86
18 Jan 2018 14:20	LUDLOW	Actinpieces	1	2.08	15.13	37.30	363.59	36.36	11.15	206.41	10.32
18 Jan 2018 15:55	WINCANTON	Jurby	1	1.38	15.49	14.47	400.89	40.09	4.13	217.56	10.88
18 Jan 2018 19:00	CHELMSFORD (A.W)	Surrey Blaze	1	1.49	15.96	19.34	415.37	41.54	5.43	221.69	11.08
19 Jan 2018 13:35	CHEPSTOW	Jammin Masters	1	1.25	16.19	10.32	434.70	43.47	2.84	227.12	11.36
19 Jan 2018 15:40	LINGFIELD (A.W)	Native Appeal	2	1.06	16.25	2.54	445.03	44.50	0.69	229.96	11.50
19 Jan 2018 16:00	MUSSELBURGH	I'm To Blame	1	1.23	16.47	9.78	447.56	44.76	2.65	230.65	11.53
19 Jan 2018 18:15	NEWCASTLE (A.W)	Cherry Oak	2	1.50	16.95	21.72	457.34	45.73	5.83	233.30	11.67
19 Jan 2018 18:45	NEWCASTLE (A.W)	Choice Encounte	2	1.44	17.36	20.03	479.07	47.91	5.26	239.13	11.96
20 Jan 2018 12:40	ASCOT	Nayati	1	1.27	17.62	12.80	499.09	49.91	3.30	244.40	12.22
20 Jan 2018 13:05	TAUNTON	Dan McGrue	1	1.19	17.80	9.24	511.89	51.19	2.35	247.70	12.38
20 Jan 2018 14:00	LINGFIELD (A.W)	Karam Albaari	3	1.60	18.37	29.70	521.13	52.11	7.50	250.05	12.50
20 Jan 2018 14:15	TAUNTON	Boite	3	1.69	19.02	36.11	550.84	55.08	8.89	257.55	12.88
20 Jan 2018 15:25	TAUNTON	Brianstorm	1	1.15	19.16	8.36	586.95	58.69	2.00	266.44	13.32
20 Jan 2018 15:35	ASCOT	Un De Sceaux	1	1.24	19.40	13.57	595.31	59.53	3.22	268.43	13.42

THE HORSE RACING PLACE BET INVESTMENT STRATEGY

Date	Course	Horse								
20 Jan 2018 18:45	CHELMSFORD (A.W)	Sweet Symphony	3	1.55	19.92	31.81	608.88	60.89	7.47	271.65	13.58
20 Jan 2018 19:45	CHELMSFORD (A.W)	Spinning Melody	1	1.51	20.40	31.04	640.70	64.07	7.12	279.13	13.96
20 Jan 2018 20:15	CHELMSFORD (A.W)	Spare Parts	3	1.45	20.83	28.72	671.74	67.17	6.44	286.24	14.31
21 Jan 2018 13:10	FONTWELL	Lisp	1	1.10	20.93	6.65	700.46	70.05	1.46	292.68	14.63
21 Jan 2018 15:10	FONTWELL	Melrose Boy	1	1.07	20.99	4.70	707.11	70.71	1.03	294.15	14.71
21 Jan 2018 15:25	CHELMSFORD (A.W)	Jack Bear	1	1.81	19.99	54.77	711.81	71.18	11.95	295.18	14.76
21 Jan 2018 16:10	FONTWELL	The Flying Sofa	0	1.22	18.99	-76.66	766.59	76.66	-15.36	307.13	15.36
22 Jan 2018 13:55	FAKENHAM	Rio Quinto	2	1.26	19.24	-68.99	689.93	68.99	-14.59	291.77	14.59
22 Jan 2018 16:20	WOLVERHAMPTON	Ray Purchase	2	1.43	19.65	25.37	620.94	62.09	5.96	277.19	13.86
22 Jan 2018 16:50	WOLVERHAMPTON	Cross Counter	1	1.11	19.75	6.75	646.30	64.63	1.56	283.15	14.16
22 Jan 2018 17:20	WOLVERHAMPTON	Big Time Maybe	0	1.45	18.75	27.92	653.05	65.31	6.41	284.70	14.24
23 Jan 2018 13:10	WETHERBY	Solo Saxophone	1	1.41	19.14	-68.10	680.97	68.10	-14.56	291.11	14.56
23 Jan 2018 14:05	LEICESTER	Arian	2	1.40	19.52	23.29	612.88	61.29	5.53	276.55	13.83
23 Jan 2018 14:40	LEICESTER	Lastbutnotleast	0	1.23	18.52	13.90	636.16	63.62	3.24	282.08	14.10
23 Jan 2018 14:55	WETHERBY	Final Fling	1	1.84	19.32	-65.01	650.06	65.01	-14.27	285.33	14.27
24 Jan 2018 13:20	CATTERICK	Jaunty Flyer	1	1.15	19.47	8.34	585.06	58.51	2.03	271.06	13.55
24 Jan 2018 13:30	LINGFIELD (A.W)	Power And Peace	1	1.16	19.62	9.02	593.40	59.34	2.18	273.09	13.65
24 Jan 2018 15:00	CATTERICK	Bentelimar	1	1.21	19.82	12.02	602.42	60.24	2.89	275.28	13.76
24 Jan 2018 15:45	LINGFIELD (A.W)	Galloway Hills	2	1.52	20.31	30.35	614.44	61.44	7.23	278.17	13.91
25 Jan 2018 12:45	KELSO	Un Guet Apens	1	1.63	20.91	38.59	644.79	64.48	8.99	285.40	14.27
25 Jan 2018 13:35	SOUTHWELL (A.W)	Cool Spirit	1	1.15	21.05	9.74	683.38	68.34	2.21	294.39	14.72
25 Jan 2018 14:45	SOUTHWELL (A.W)	Maifalki	3	1.42	21.44	27.66	693.11	69.31	6.23	296.60	14.83
25 Jan 2018 14:55	KELSO	Cool Mix	1	1.08	21.52	5.48	720.77	72.08	1.21	302.83	15.14
26 Jan 2018 13:25	DONCASTER	Perfect Harmony	2	1.37	21.87	25.53	726.25	72.62	5.62	304.04	15.20
26 Jan 2018 13:35	HUNTINGDON	Django Django	1	1.27	22.13	19.28	751.78	75.18	4.18	309.66	15.48
26 Jan 2018 13:45	LINGFIELD (A.W)	Ambient	2	1.18	22.30	13.19	771.06	77.11	2.82	313.85	15.69
26 Jan 2018 14:30	DONCASTER	Nube Negra	1	1.07	22.37	5.22	784.24	78.42	1.11	316.67	15.83
26 Jan 2018 19:45	KEMPTON	Wiff Waff	0	1.41	21.37	30.75	789.46	78.95	6.51	317.78	15.89
27 Jan 2018 12:40	CHELTENHAM	Apple's Shakira	1	1.09	21.45	-82.02	820.21	82.02	-16.21	324.29	16.21
27 Jan 2018 13:30	DONCASTER	Sceau Royal	1	1.19	21.63	13.32	738.19	73.82	2.93	308.08	15.40
27 Jan 2018 14:20	UTTOXETER	Crank Em Up	2	1.74	21.34	52.07	751.51	79.48	11.61	311.60	15.53
27 Jan 2018 15:15	DONCASTER	L'Ami Serge	3	1.57	22.88	43.56	804.34	80.43	9.19	322.51	16.13
27 Jan 2018 19:15	KEMPTON (A.W)	Choice Encounter	3	1.49	22.71	30.47	847.90	84.79	8.13	331.70	16.59
28 Jan 2018 13:40	SEDGEFIELD	Beau Bay	1	1.51	22.34	42.99	887.37	88.74	8.67	339.83	16.99
28 Jan 2018 14:40	SEDGEFIELD	Ascendant	1	1.13	22.47	11.49	930.36	93.04	2.27	348.50	17.42
29 Jan 2018 14:40	HEREFORD	Snapdragon Fire	2	1.35	22.79	31.32	941.85	94.19	6.14	350.76	17.54
29 Jan 2018 18:00	WOLVERHAMPTON	Montague	1	1.23	23.01	21.26	973.17	97.32	4.10	356.90	17.84
29 Jan 2018 19:30	WOLVERHAMPTON	Abe Lincoln	1	1.09	23.09	8.50	994.43	99.44	1.62	361.00	18.05
30 Jan 2018 13:35	NEWCASTLE	Petticoat Tails	1	1.42	23.49	40.02	1002.93	100.29	7.62	362.63	18.13
30 Jan 2018 14:15	SOUTHWELL (A.W)	Kommander Kirk	2	1.97	24.41	96.11	1042.95	104.30	17.96	370.24	18.51
30 Jan 2018 14:40	SOUTHWELL (A.W)	Love Rat	2	1.55	24.93	59.52	1139.06	113.91	10.68	388.20	19.41
30 Jan 2018 15:15	LINGFIELD	Lostnfound	2	1.40	25.31	45.55	1198.57	119.86	7.98	398.88	19.94
30 Jan 2018 16:25	SOUTHWELL (A.W)	Sooqaan	1	1.47	25.76	55.55	1244.12	124.41	9.56	406.85	20.34
31 Jan 2018 13:15	LEICESTER	Springtown Lake	1	0.00	25.76	-123.47	1299.67	129.97	-20.82	416.41	20.82
31 Jan 2018 13:25	CHELMSFORD (A.W)	My Amigo	2	1.52	26.28	58.10	1176.20	117.62	10.29	395.59	19.78
31 Jan 2018 13:45	LEICESTER	Head To The Star	2	1.66	26.82	77.39	1234.31	123.43	13.39	405.88	20.29
31 Jan 2018 14:50	LEICESTER	Ballyarthur	3	1.21	25.88	26.17	1311.70	131.17	4.40	419.27	20.96
31 Jan 2018 15:35	CHELMSFORD (A.W)	Danzan	1	1.05	25.93	6.35	1337.87	133.79	1.06	423.68	21.18
31 Jan 2018 17:15	NEWCASTLE (A.W)	Furni Factors	2	1.48	26.38	61.30	1344.22	134.42	10.19	424.73	21.24
01 Feb 2018 13:20	WINCANTON	Molineaux	1	1.14	26.51	18.69	1405.52	140.55	3.04	434.93	21.75
01 Feb 2018 13:30	SOUTHWELL (A.W)	Something Lucky	3	1.51	27.00	69.00	1424.21	142.42	11.17	437.97	21.90
01 Feb 2018 14:05	SOUTHWELL (A.W)	Dream Serenade	1	1.46	27.44	65.25	1493.21	149.32	10.33	449.14	22.46
01 Feb 2018 14:40	SOUTHWELL (A.W)	Ray Purchase	1	1.11	27.54	16.29	1558.47	155.85	2.53	459.47	22.97
01 Feb 2018 15:00	WINCANTON	Captain Cattisto	1	1.31	27.84	46.38	1574.75	157.48	7.16	462.00	23.10
01 Feb 2018 15:25	TOWCESTER	Dr Des	1	1.09	27.92	13.86	1621.13	162.11	2.11	469.16	23.46
01 Feb 2018 16:35	TOWCESTER	Cafe Au Lait	2	1.45	28.35	69.90	1634.99	163.50	10.60	471.27	23.56
01 Feb 2018 16:45	WINCANTON	Hideaway Vic	2	1.15	28.49	24.29	1704.89	170.49	3.61	481.87	24.09
02 Feb 2018 13:10	CHEPSTOW	Don't Ask	2	1.11	28.60	18.07	1729.18	172.92	2.77	485.49	24.27
02 Feb 2018 14:15	CHEPSTOW	Rock My Style	1	1.36	28.94	59.76	1747.25	174.72	8.79	488.16	24.41
02 Feb 2018 14:35	LINGFIELD (A.W)	Craving	2	1.58	29.49	99.57	1807.01	180.70	14.41	496.95	24.85
02 Feb 2018 15:05	LINGFIELD (A.W)	Watersmeet	1	1.12	29.60	21.73	1906.57	190.66	3.07	511.36	25.57
02 Feb 2018 13:40	CATTERICK	Timon's Tara	1	1.64	28.60	117.24	1928.31	192.83	16.46	514.42	25.72
02 Feb 2018 16:35	CATTERICK	Derrynane	2	1.31	28.90	60.24	2045.55	204.55	8.23	530.89	26.54
03 Feb 2018 12:55	MUSSELBURGH	Coup De Pinceau	1	1.32	29.20	64.02	2105.79	210.58	8.63	539.12	26.96
03 Feb 2018 13:35	WETHERBY	Kayf Blanco	2	1.72	20.88	140.41	2169.81	216.98	19.72	547.74	27.39
03 Feb 2018 14:00	LINGFIELD (A.W)	Kashy	1	1.58	30.38	114.32	2318.22	231.82	14.75	567.46	28.37
03 Feb 2018 14:10	WETHERBY	Robin Waters	1	1.08	30.46	18.49	2432.74	243.27	2.33	582.21	29.11
03 Feb 2018 15:20	WETHERBY	Red Rising	1	1.35	30.80	81.50	2451.23	245.12	10.23	584.54	29.23
03 Feb 2018 16:05	LINGFIELD (A.W)	Galway Jack	1	0.00	30.80	-249.13	2532.73	253.27	-29.74	594.77	29.74
03 Feb 2018 16:15	LINGFIELD (A.W)	Master Archer	2	1.22	31.00	47.91	2292.12	229.21	6.22	565.03	28.25
03 Feb 2018 16:20	MUSSELBURGH	Wonderful Charm	1	1.17	31.16	37.79	2340.03	234.00	4.86	571.25	28.56
04 Feb 2018 13:25	MUSSELBURGH	We Have A Dream	1	1.12	31.28	27.11	2377.82	237.78	3.46	576.10	28.81
04 Feb 2018 16:15	TAUNTON	Vocaliser	1	1.64	31.88	146.22	2404.93	240.49	18.55	579.56	28.98
05 Feb 2018 14:15	NEWCASTLE	Undefined Beauty	2	0.00	30.88	-242.36	2551.15	255.11	-29.91	598.11	29.91
05 Feb 2018 15:35	SOUTHWELL	Global Citizen	1	1.10	30.98	21.93	2308.79	230.88	2.84	568.20	28.41
05 Feb 2018 16:20	NEWCASTLE	Absolutely Dylan	2	1.09	31.06	19.93	2330.72	233.07	2.57	571.04	28.55
05 Feb 2018 18:15	WOLVERHAMPTON	Arcanada	1	1.17	31.23	37.96	2350.65	235.06	4.88	573.61	28.68
06 Feb 2018 16:40	SOUTHWELL (A.W)	Star Ascending	1	1.27	31.48	61.27	2388.61	238.86	7.81	578.49	28.92
07 Feb 2018 13:55	CHELMSFORD (A.W)	Dragon Mall	1	1.09	31.56	20.95	2449.88	244.99	2.64	586.30	29.31
07 Feb 2018 15:30	CHELMSFORD (A.W)	Volturnus	1	1.31	31.86	72.77	2470.83	247.08	9.13	588.94	29.45
07 Feb 2018 16:55	WOLVERHAMPTON	Temeraire	3	1.24	32.09	57.99	2543.59	254.36	7.18	598.06	29.90
08 Feb 2018 14:55	TOWCESTER	Red Indian	2	1.19	32.27	46.96	2601.59	260.16	5.75	605.24	30.26
08 Feb 2018 15:25	TOWCESTER	Tommy Rapper	1	1.33	32.59	83.03	2648.54	264.85	10.08	610.99	30.55
09 Feb 2018 13:30	CHELMSFORD (A.W)	Nice Shot	1	1.06	32.65	15.57	2731.58	273.16	1.86	621.07	31.05
09 Feb 2018 15:45	BANGOR-ON-DEE	Happy Diva	1	1.24	32.88	62.63	2747.15	274.71	7.48	622.94	31.15
09 Feb 2018 17:45	NEWCASTLE (A.W)	Lord Caprio	1	1.36	33.22	96.09	2809.78	280.98	11.35	630.41	31.52
09 Feb 2018 18:15	NEWCASTLE (A.W)	Gronkowski	1	1.06	33.27	16.56	2905.87	290.59	1.93	641.76	32.09
10 Feb 2018 13:30	WARWICK	Rio Quinto	2	1.51	33.57	86.07	2922.44	292.24	9.98	643.68	32.18
10 Feb 2018 14:20	LINGFIELD (A.W)	Gabriel The Devil	3	1.17	33.73	48.59	3008.50	300.85	5.56	653.66	32.68

THE HORSE RACING PLACE BET INVESTMENT STRATEGY

Date	Course	Horse		Odds	%	P/L	Bank	Col	Stake	Run	Tot
10 Feb 2018 14:25	NEWBURY	Native River	1	1.23	33.95	66.80	3057.09	305.71	7.58	659.22	32.96
10 Feb 2018 15:40	UTTOXETER	Game On	1	1.33	34.26	97.93	3123.89	312.39	11.00	666.80	33.34
10 Feb 2018 15:50	WARWICK	Just A Thought	2	1.73	34.95	223.43	3221.82	322.18	24.74	677.80	33.89
10 Feb 2018 16:20	WARWICK	Solighoster	1	0.00	34.95	-327.30	3445.26	344.53	-35.13	702.54	35.13
10 Feb 2018 19:45	WOLVERHAMPTON	Atletico	2	1.46	35.39	136.25	3117.96	311.80	15.35	667.41	33.37
11 Feb 2018 13:50	AYR	Just Don't Ask	1	1.07	35.45	21.64	3254.21	325.42	2.39	682.76	34.14
11 Feb 2018 14:30	EXETER	Mercenaire	2	1.39	35.82	121.37	3275.85	327.59	13.36	685.15	34.26
11 Feb 2018 14:55	AYR	Grand Morning	1	1.31	36.12	100.05	3397.22	339.72	10.83	698.51	34.93
11 Feb 2018 15:25	AYR	Progress Drive	1	1.29	36.40	96.35	3497.27	349.73	10.29	709.34	35.47
11 Feb 2018 16:10	EXETER	Elegant Escape	1	1.19	36.58	64.86	3593.62	359.36	6.84	719.63	35.98
11 Feb 2018 17:10	EXETER	Time To Move On	1	1.12	36.69	41.71	3658.49	365.85	4.36	726.46	36.32
12 Feb 2018 14:00	CATTERICK	LuckIme	1	1.05	36.74	17.58	3700.19	370.02	1.83	730.82	36.54
12 Feb 2018 14:15	PLUMPTON	Kaloci	1	1.09	36.83	31.79	3717.77	371.78	3.30	732.65	36.63
12 Feb 2018 17:10	WOLVERHAMPTON	Crown Walk	2	1.09	36.91	32.06	3749.56	374.96	3.31	735.94	36.80
13 Feb 2018 16:00	SOUTHWELL (A.W)	Mister Music	1	2.22	38.07	438.29	3781.61	378.16	45.09	739.26	36.96
13 Feb 2018 16:30	SOUTHWELL (A.W)	Volatile	1	1.47	38.52	188.42	4219.90	421.99	18.43	784.35	39.22
14 Feb 2018 14:10	TOWCESTER	Cafe Au Lait	3	1.47	38.96	196.83	4408.32	440.83	18.87	802.78	40.14
14 Feb 2018 14:30	MUSSELBURGH	Silver Concorde	1	0.00	38.96	-437.49	4605.15	460.52	-41.08	821.65	41.08
14 Feb 2018 15:00	MUSSELBURGH	Divine Spear	2	1.10	39.06	39.59	4167.66	416.77	3.90	780.57	39.03
14 Feb 2018 15:20	LINGFIELD (A.W)	Snaffled	1	1.27	39.31	107.92	4207.26	420.73	10.59	784.47	39.22
14 Feb 2018 15:50	LINGFIELD (A.W)	Red Verdon	1	1.10	39.41	40.99	4315.17	431.52	3.98	795.06	39.75
14 Feb 2018 16:30	MUSSELBURGH	Nefyn Bay	1	2.38	40.72	571.09	4356.17	435.62	55.13	799.03	39.95
15 Feb 2018 13:40	LEICESTER	Glance Back	1	1.69	41.37	322.98	4927.26	492.73	29.47	854.17	42.71
15 Feb 2018 13:55	KELSO	Mcgowan's Pass	3	1.19	41.55	94.77	5250.24	525.02	8.39	883.64	44.18
15 Feb 2018 14:05	FONTWELL	Night Of Glory	1	1.28	41.81	142.18	5345.01	534.50	12.49	892.03	44.60
15 Feb 2018 14:15	LEICESTER	Dylanseoghan	2	1.82	42.59	427.45	5487.19	548.72	37.09	904.52	45.23
15 Feb 2018 14:55	FONTWELL	Rothman	1	1.27	42.85	151.71	5914.64	591.46	12.71	941.61	47.08
15 Feb 2018 15:20	LEICESTER	Tree Of Liberty	1	1.06	42.91	34.58	6066.35	606.63	2.86	954.32	47.72
15 Feb 2018 16:55	FONTWELL	Scorpion Haze	2	1.55	41.91	318.77	6100.93	610.09	26.32	957.18	47.86
15 Feb 2018 19:00	CHELMSFORD (A.W)	Beautiful Memory	1	1.13	42.03	79.28	6419.70	641.97	6.39	983.50	49.18
15 Feb 2018 20:30	CHELMSFORD (A.W)	Be Bold	2	1.69	42.69	426.01	6498.98	649.90	34.15	989.90	49.49
16 Feb 2018 13:40	FAKENHAM	Hurricane Rita	3	1.34	43.01	223.68	6924.99	692.50	17.41	1024.05	51.20
16 Feb 2018 14:45	FAKENHAM	Whiskey In The Jar	1	1.15	43.15	101.87	7148.67	714.87	7.81	1041.46	52.07
16 Feb 2018 15:10	LINGFIELD (A.W)	Dragon Mall	2	1.10	43.25	68.88	7250.54	725.05	5.25	1049.27	52.46
16 Feb 2018 15:20	FAKENHAM	Princeton Royale	2	2.10	44.29	764.88	7319.42	731.94	58.00	1054.51	52.73
16 Feb 2018 15:50	FAKENHAM	Calipso Collonges	1	1.04	44.33	30.72	8084.30	808.43	2.23	1112.51	55.63
17 Feb 2018 13:45	LINGFIELD (A.W)	Completion	2	1.13	44.46	100.22	8115.02	811.50	7.25	1114.74	55.74
17 Feb 2018 13:50	ASCOT	Black Corton	1	1.30	44.74	234.13	8215.24	821.52	16.83	1121.98	56.10
17 Feb 2018 14:05	HAYDOCK	Agrapart	2	1.23	44.95	184.62	8449.37	844.94	13.10	1138.81	56.94
18 Feb 2018 15:50	MARKET RASEN	Captain Chaos	1	1.14	45.09	114.83	8633.99	863.40	8.06	1151.91	57.60
19 Feb 2018 14:00	CARLISLE	Ballinslea Bridge	1	1.61	45.66	506.99	8748.82	874.88	35.38	1159.97	58.00
19 Feb 2018 16:25	LINGFIELD	Le Musee	2	1.15	45.80	131.90	9255.82	925.58	8.97	1195.35	59.77
19 Feb 2018 17:10	CARLISLE	Windsor Avenue	1	1.04	45.85	35.67	9387.71	938.77	2.41	1204.32	60.22
19 Feb 2018 17:50	KEMPTON (A.W)	American Gigolo	1	1.11	45.95	98.47	9423.39	942.34	6.64	1206.72	60.34
19 Feb 2018 19:50	KEMPTON (A.W)	Lacan	2	1.70	46.62	633.20	9521.86	952.19	42.47	1213.36	60.67
20 Feb 2018 15:00	WETHERBY	Rosmuc Relay	1	1.12	46.73	115.77	10155.06	1015.51	7.53	1255.83	62.79
20 Feb 2018 20:10	WOLVERHAMPTON	Sweet Symphony	2	1.35	47.05	341.51	10270.83	1027.08	22.11	1263.36	63.17
21 Feb 2018 15:25	NEWCASTLE (A.W)	Corinthia Knight	1	1.47	47.50	473.84	10612.34	1061.23	30.21	1285.47	64.27
21 Feb 2018 15:55	DONCASTER	Pacha Du Polder	3	1.62	46.50	652.98	11086.18	1108.62	40.79	1315.68	65.78
21 Feb 2018 16:55	NEWCASTLE (A.W)	Casey Jones	1	1.24	46.73	267.65	11739.15	1173.92	16.28	1356.47	67.82
22 Feb 2018 14:35	SOUTHWELL (A.W)	Silchester	2	1.17	46.89	193.91	12006.81	1200.68	11.67	1372.74	68.64
22 Feb 2018 15:10	SOUTHWELL (A.W)	Ray Purchase	3	1.11	46.99	127.50	12200.72	1220.07	7.61	1384.41	69.22
22 Feb 2018 16:15	SOUTHWELL (A.W)	Foolaad	1	1.53	47.49	620.73	12328.21	1232.82	36.89	1392.03	69.60
22 Feb 2018 16:40	HUNTINGDON	Kincora Fort	1	1.44	47.91	541.27	12948.94	1294.89	31.44	1428.92	71.45
22 Feb 2018 17:15	HUNTINGDON	Voie Dans Voie	1	1.11	48.01	140.97	13490.20	1349.02	8.03	1460.35	73.02
22 Feb 2018 19:30	CHELMSFORD (A.W)	Danzan	1	1.05	48.06	64.75	13631.18	1363.12	3.67	1468.38	73.42
23 Feb 2018 15:10	EXETER	Molineaux	2	1.17	48.22	221.19	13695.92	1369.59	12.51	1472.06	73.60
23 Feb 2018 18:15	WOLVERHAMPTON	Navajo Star	2	1.52	48.71	687.51	13917.11	1391.71	38.60	1484.57	74.23
24 Feb 2018 13:50	KEMPTON	Cyrname	1	1.14	48.85	194.24	14604.62	1460.46	10.66	1523.17	76.16
24 Feb 2018 14:15	NEWCASTLE	Lady Buttons	1	1.22	49.06	309.30	14798.86	1479.89	16.87	1533.83	76.69
24 Feb 2018 15:20	NEWCASTLE	Raised On Grazed	1	1.10	49.15	143.53	15108.16	1510.82	7.75	1550.70	77.54
24 Feb 2018 18:45	WOLVERHAMPTON	Iconic Belle	2	1.42	49.55	608.54	15251.68	1525.17	32.73	1558.45	77.92
25 Feb 2018 15:30	SOUTHWELL	Kansas City Chief	2	1.53	50.06	798.56	15860.23	1586.02	42.17	1591.18	79.56
26 Feb 2018 14:30	PLUMPTON	Holbrook Park	1	1.16	50.21	253.21	16658.79	1665.88	13.07	1633.35	81.67
26 Feb 2018 15:50	AYR	Looksnowtlikebr	1	1.12	50.32	192.80	16912.00	1691.20	9.88	1646.41	82.32
26 Feb 2018 16:00	LINGFIELD (A.W)	Sotomayor	1	1.36	50.66	584.98	17104.80	1710.48	29.81	1656.29	82.81
26 Feb 2018 16:10	PLUMPTON	Greyed A	1	1.30	50.95	504.16	17689.78	1768.98	25.29	1686.11	84.31
26 Feb 2018 16:20	AYR	One For Harry	3	1.50	49.95	864.21	18193.94	1819.39	42.78	1711.40	85.57
26 Feb 2018 17:30	AYR	Black Pirate	1	1.06	50.01	108.63	19058.15	1905.82	5.26	1754.18	87.71
26 Feb 2018 17:45	WOLVERHAMPTON	Ty Rock Brandy	1	1.20	50.20	364.17	19166.79	1916.68	17.59	1759.45	87.97
26 Feb 2018 18:45	WOLVERHAMPTON	Legal History	3	1.45	49.20	834.95	19530.95	1953.10	39.98	1777.04	88.85
26 Feb 2018 19:45	WOLVERHAMPTON	Inn The Bull	1	1.27	49.45	522.39	20365.90	2036.59	24.53	1817.02	90.85
26 Feb 2018 20:15	WOLVERHAMPTON	Atletico	2	1.66	50.08	1309.70	20888.29	2088.83	60.77	1841.55	92.08
27 Feb 2018 14:15	CHELMSFORD (A.W)	I Was Only Joking	2	1.24	50.31	506.11	22197.98	2219.80	22.83	1902.32	95.12
27 Feb 2018 14:30	LINGFIELD (A.W)	Walk In The Sun	1	1.05	50.35	107.84	22704.10	2270.41	4.81	1925.15	96.26
27 Feb 2018 15:45	CHELMSFORD (A.W)	Mambo Dancer	1	1.58	50.90	1256.94	22811.94	2281.19	55.97	1929.97	96.50
27 Feb 2018 16:15	CHELMSFORD (A.W)	Shamshon	2	1.06	50.96	137.19	24068.88	2406.89	5.96	1985.93	99.30
28 Feb 2018 15:20	WOLVERHAMPTON	King Kevin	3	1.26	49.96	597.89	24206.07	2420.61	25.89	1991.89	99.59
28 Feb 2018 16:55	WOLVERHAMPTON	Dubai Acclaim	1	1.27	50.22	636.22	24803.96	2480.40	27.24	2017.79	100.89
02 Mar 2018 15:20	SOUTHWELL (A.W)	Man Look	3	1.15	50.37	362.52	25440.19	2544.02	15.34	2045.03	102.25
03 Mar 2018 14:05	NEWCASTLE (A.W)	Bournville	1	1.08	50.44	196.10	25802.71	2580.27	8.24	2060.36	103.02
03 Mar 2018 15:50	NEWCASTLE (A.W)	Forest Bihan	1	1.10	50.54	246.99	25998.81	2599.88	10.34	2068.61	103.43
03 Mar 2018 16:35	LINGFIELD (A.W)	Porrima	1	1.50	51.01	1246.68	26245.80	2624.58	51.97	2078.95	103.95
03 Mar 2018 17:45	CHELMSFORD (A.W)	Kodiac Express	2	1.36	51.35	940.24	27492.47	2749.25	38.36	2130.92	106.55
03 Mar 2018 18:15	CHELMSFORD (A.W)	Jellmood	1	1.05	51.40	135.06	28432.72	2843.27	5.42	2169.28	108.46
04 Mar 2018 14:15	SOUTHWELL (A.W)	Kingstreet Lady	3	1.44	51.82	1194.13	28567.77	2856.78	47.84	2174.70	108.74
04 Mar 2018 14:45	SOUTHWELL (A.W)	Dawn Dancer	2	1.10	51.92	282.74	29761.90	2976.19	11.11	2222.55	111.13
04 Mar 2018 15:50	SOUTHWELL (A.W)	Best Tamayuz	3	1.36	52.25	1027.53	30044.64	3004.46	40.21	2233.66	111.68
05 Mar 2018 14:10	LINGFIELD (A.W)	Skyline	3	1.12	52.37	354.22	31072.17	3107.22	13.64	2273.86	113.69

THE HORSE RACING PLACE BET INVESTMENT STRATEGY

Date	Course	Horse	Pos	Odds	Col6	Col7	Col8	Col9	Col10	Col11	Col12
05 Mar 2018 14:30	KEMPTON (A.W)	Tommy Silver	2	1.05	52.42	149.28	31426.39	3142.64	5.72	2287.51	114.38
05 Mar 2018 14:40	LINGFIELD	Kupatana	1	1.19	52.60	569.94	31575.67	3157.57	21.79	2293.23	114.66
05 Mar 2018 14:50	SOUTHWELL	Peppay Le Pugh	2	1.97	53.52	2962.22	32145.61	3214.56	112.28	2315.01	115.75
05 Mar 2018 16:25	SOUTHWELL	Tomkevi	1	2.00	54.47	3335.24	35107.82	3510.78	121.36	2427.29	121.36
05 Mar 2018 16:50	LINGFIELD	Brother Norphin	2	2.26	55.67	4601.64	38443.07	3844.31	160.57	2548.66	127.43
05 Mar 2018 18:15	WOLVERHAMPTON	Captain Cat	1	1.25	55.91	1022.31	43044.70	4304.47	33.87	2709.22	135.46
05 Mar 2018 20:15	WOLVERHAMPTON	Black Sails	2	1.12	56.02	502.36	44067.01	4406.70	16.46	2743.09	137.15
07 Mar 2018 14:20	CATTERICK	Verni	1	1.21	56.21	889.16	44569.38	4456.94	28.98	2759.54	137.98
07 Mar 2018 15:10	FONTWELL	Casterly Rock	3	1.15	56.36	647.78	45458.54	4545.85	20.91	2788.52	139.43
07 Mar 2018 15:30	LINGFIELD (A.W)	De Medici	3	1.15	56.50	657.02	46106.32	4610.63	21.07	2809.43	140.47
07 Mar 2018 18:40	KEMPTON (A.W)	Herecomesthesu	1	1.35	56.83	1554.88	46763.34	4676.33	49.53	2830.50	141.53
08 Mar 2018 15:00	SOUTHWELL (A.W)	Craving	1	1.03	56.86	137.71	48318.22	4831.82	4.32	2880.04	144.00
08 Mar 2018 16:30	CARLISLE	Louse Talk	1	1.09	56.95	414.30	48455.93	4845.59	12.98	2884.36	144.22
08 Mar 2018 17:20	WINCANTON	Zee Man	2	1.26	57.20	1207.09	48870.22	4887.02	37.67	2897.34	144.87
08 Mar 2018 17:35	CARLISLE	Shantaluze	3	1.44	56.20	2093.23	50077.32	5007.73	64.57	2935.00	146.75
08 Mar 2018 18:15	NEWCASTLE (A.W)	Night Castle	1	1.42	56.59	2081.60	52170.55	5217.05	62.99	2999.57	149.98
09 Mar 2018 14:00	SANDOWN	Brianstorm	1	1.06	56.65	309.24	54252.15	5425.22	9.19	3062.56	153.13
09 Mar 2018 14:10	LEICESTER	Bollin Ace	1	1.12	56.76	622.00	54561.39	5456.14	18.43	3071.75	153.59
09 Mar 2018 16:00	AYR	Lake View Lad	2	1.37	57.11	1939.70	55183.39	5518.34	57.17	3090.18	154.51
09 Mar 2018 18:15	NEWCASTLE (A.W)	Furni Factors	3	1.73	57.81	3961.49	57123.09	5712.31	114.88	3147.35	157.37
09 Mar 2018 20:45	NEWCASTLE (A.W)	Windforpower	1	1.57	58.35	3307.73	61084.57	6108.46	92.97	3262.23	163.11
10 Mar 2018 14:10	AYR	Uppertown Princ	1	1.04	58.39	244.69	64392.30	6439.23	6.71	3355.20	167.76
10 Mar 2018 14:40	WOLVERHAMPTON	Intern	1	1.09	58.47	552.65	64636.99	6463.70	15.13	3361.91	168.10
10 Mar 2018 15:50	WOLVERHAMPTON	Ojala	3	2.15	57.47	7121.97	65189.64	6518.96	194.18	3377.04	168.85
10 Mar 2018 16:00	HEREFORD	Just Your Type	1	1.17	57.64	1167.83	72311.61	7231.16	30.36	3571.22	178.56
10 Mar 2018 17:10	HEREFORD	Burrows Edge	1	1.04	57.68	279.22	73479.44	7347.94	7.20	3601.58	180.08
10 Mar 2018 17:35	AYR	Precious Cargo	1	1.07	57.74	490.50	73758.66	7375.87	12.63	3608.78	180.44
10 Mar 2018 19:15	CHELMSFORD (A.W)	Jazirat	1	1.43	58.15	3033.08	74249.16	7424.92	77.86	3621.41	181.07
10 Mar 2018 20:15	CHELMSFORD (A.W)	Broderie	1	1.24	58.39	1762.04	77282.24	7728.22	44.39	3699.27	184.96
11 Mar 2018 14:20	WARWICK	Piton Pete	1	1.10	58.48	750.92	79044.27	7904.43	18.72	3743.66	187.18
12 Mar 2018 14:20	PLUMPTON	Larry	1	1.06	58.54	454.83	79795.19	7979.52	11.29	3762.38	188.12
12 Mar 2018 14:50	PLUMPTON	Duhallow Lad	1	2.40	59.87	10673.25	80250.03	8025.00	264.16	3773.67	188.68
12 Mar 2018 16:50	PLUMPTON	Lubatic	2	1.31	60.16	2677.69	90923.28	9092.33	62.59	4037.82	201.89
12 Mar 2018 17:10	TAUNTON	Rosy World	3	1.23	60.38	2045.18	93600.97	9360.10	47.15	4100.41	205.02
12 Mar 2018 19:45	CHELMSFORD (A.W)	Stone Of Destiny	1	1.02	60.40	181.73	95646.15	9564.62	4.15	4147.57	207.38
13 Mar 2018 15:30	CHELTENHAM	Buveur D'Air	1	1.31	60.69	2822.13	95827.88	9582.79	64.35	4151.71	207.59
13 Mar 2018 15:45	SOUTHWELL (A.W)	Haddaf	1	1.20	60.88	1874.35	98650.01	9865.00	42.16	4216.06	210.80
13 Mar 2018 15:55	SEDGEFIELD	Instant Replay	1	1.20	61.08	1909.96	100524.36	10052.44	42.58	4258.23	212.91
13 Mar 2018 17:00	SOUTHWELL (A.W)	Ochos Rios	3	1.32	61.38	3114.00	102434.32	10243.43	68.81	4300.81	215.04
13 Mar 2018 17:10	SEDGEFIELD	Peters Cousin	2	1.06	61.44	601.63	105548.33	10554.83	13.11	4369.62	218.48
13 Mar 2018 18:45	NEWCASTLE (A.W)	Regina Pacis	1	1.15	61.58	1512.64	106149.95	10615.00	32.87	4382.73	219.14
14 Mar 2018 13:55	SOUTHWELL (A.W)	Scribner Creek	2	2.01	62.55	10330.23	107662.59	10766.26	222.99	4415.60	220.78
14 Mar 2018 14:35	SOUTHWELL (A.W)	Line House	1	1.62	63.14	6949.78	117992.81	11799.28	143.80	4638.59	231.93
14 Mar 2018 15:05	HUNTINGDON	Chandos Belle	1	2.17	64.25	13887.37	124942.59	12494.26	279.77	4782.38	239.12
14 Mar 2018 18:45	WOLVERHAMPTON	Seasearch	1	1.58	64.80	7649.53	138829.96	13883.00	146.80	5062.15	253.11
14 Mar 2018 19:15	WOLVERHAMPTON	Bowditch	1	1.11	64.90	1530.71	146479.49	14647.95	28.65	5208.96	260.45
15 Mar 2018 13:30	CHELTENHAM	Terrefort	2	1.80	65.67	11248.78	148010.20	14801.02	209.50	5237.60	261.88
15 Mar 2018 13:45	HEXHAM	Cornerstone Lad	2	0.00	65.57	-15129.60	159258.97	15925.90	-272.36	5447.11	272.36
15 Mar 2018 14:25	HEXHAM	Nelly La Rue	1	1.43	66.08	5887.68	144129.37	14412.94	111.26	5174.75	258.74
15 Mar 2018 14:50	CHELTENHAM	Un De Sceaux	1	1.47	66.52	6698.26	150017.06	15001.71	124.22	5286.01	264.30
15 Mar 2018 17:15	TOWCESTER	Hazel Hill	1	1.12	66.64	1786.55	156715.32	15671.53	32.46	5410.23	270.51
15 Mar 2018 19:30	CHELMSFORD (A.W)	Aquarium	1	1.44	67.06	6625.38	158501.87	15850.19	119.74	5442.69	272.13
16 Mar 2018 12:05	MUSSELBURGH	Bedrock	1	1.12	67.18	1882.45	165127.25	16512.73	33.37	5562.43	278.12
16 Mar 2018 12:40	MUSSELBURGH	Middlebrow	2	1.21	67.37	3331.84	167009.70	16700.97	58.76	5595.81	279.79
16 Mar 2018 14:00	FAKENHAM	Ascendant	1	1.11	67.47	1780.07	170341.55	17034.15	31.10	5654.56	282.73
16 Mar 2018 14:30	MUSSELBURGH	Attention Please	3	1.97	66.47	15861.01	172121.61	17212.16	275.75	5685.66	284.28
16 Mar 2018 14:50	CHELTENHAM	Santini	3	2.20	67.62	21430.02	187982.62	18798.26	357.69	5961.42	298.07
16 Mar 2018 15:20	FAKENHAM	Weebill	1	1.13	67.74	2586.25	209412.64	20941.26	41.07	6319.10	315.96
16 Mar 2018 17:00	LINGFIELD (A.W)	Freebe Rocks	1	1.63	68.34	12688.13	211998.89	21199.89	200.35	6360.18	318.01
16 Mar 2018 18:15	WOLVERHAMPTON	Carpet Time	1	1.10	68.43	2134.53	224687.02	22468.70	32.80	6560.52	328.03
17 Mar 2018 13:40	FONTWELL	Big Robin	1	1.38	68.80	8188.26	226821.55	22682.15	125.27	6593.33	329.67
17 Mar 2018 15:50	KEMPTON	Chosen Path	1	1.18	68.90	2455.85	235009.80	23500.98	36.95	6718.60	335.93
17 Mar 2018 16:10	UTTOXETER	I Just Know	1	1.57	69.44	12858.77	237465.66	23746.57	201.62	6755.55	337.78
17 Mar 2018 17:20	UTTOXETER	Whiskey In The Ja	2	1.16	69.59	3804.93	250324.42	25032.44	55.58	6948.08	347.40
20 Mar 2018 14:30	WETHERBY	Sainte Ladylime	1	0.00	69.59	-24142.79	254129.35	25412.94	-360.18	7003.67	350.18
20 Mar 2018 17:15	UTTOXETER	Good Boy Bobby	1	1.12	69.72	2810.31	229907.00	22990.71	43.25	6653.43	332.67
20 Mar 2018 17:35	NEWCASTLE (A.W)	Dubawi Fifty	3	1.29	68.72	6414.40	232827.41	23282.74	97.10	6696.73	334.84
20 Mar 2018 18:05	NEWCASTLE (A.W)	Bobby K	1	1.28	68.98	6363.83	239241.80	23924.18	95.11	6793.84	339.69
21 Mar 2018 14:30	SOUTHWELL (A.W)	Epitaph	1	1.51	69.46	11899.59	245605.63	24560.56	175.67	6889.78	344.46
21 Mar 2018 14:40	HAYDOCK	Skewiff	1	1.47	69.91	11497.61	257505.22	25750.52	166.02	7064.62	353.23
21 Mar 2018 15:40	SOUTHWELL (A.W)	Holiday Magic	1	1.92	68.91	23510.85	269002.83	26900.28	332.61	7230.64	361.53
21 Mar 2018 16:55	HAYDOCK	Calipso Collonge	1	1.18	69.08	5001.98	292515.68	29251.37	68.07	7563.25	378.16
21 Mar 2018 18:15	WOLVERHAMPTON	Mandalayan	1	1.36	69.43	10175.04	297515.66	29751.57	137.36	7631.31	381.57
22 Mar 2018 14:30	LUDLOW	Michael's Mount	1	1.09	69.51	2630.76	307690.70	30769.07	34.96	7768.68	388.43
22 Mar 2018 14:40	WOLVERHAMPTON	Global Academy	1	1.07	69.58	2063.64	310321.46	31032.15	27.31	7803.64	390.18
22 Mar 2018 14:50	CHEPSTOW	Kupatana	1	1.15	69.72	4451.49	312385.09	31238.51	58.73	7830.95	391.55
22 Mar 2018 15:00	LUDLOW	Tree Of Liberty	1	1.07	69.79	2106.96	316836.58	31683.66	27.61	7889.68	394.48
22 Mar 2018 15:25	CHEPSTOW	Chooseyourweap	3	1.37	68.79	11210.87	318943.54	31894.35	146.47	7917.30	395.86
22 Mar 2018 16:10	LUDLOW	Tornado In Milan	1	1.42	69.19	13173.16	330154.41	33015.44	169.34	8063.77	403.19
22 Mar 2018 16:35	CHEPSTOW	Minellatillmornin	1	1.72	69.87	23483.61	343327.57	34332.76	296.38	8233.10	411.66
22 Mar 2018 18:00	WOLVERHAMPTON	Scribner Creek	1	1.40	70.25	13938.82	366811.18	36681.12	170.59	8529.50	426.47
22 Mar 2018 18:45	CHELMSFORD (A.W)	Nonios	1	1.39	70.62	14106.79	380750.00	38075.00	169.65	8700.09	435.00
22 Mar 2018 19:45	CHELMSFORD (A.W)	Kion	1	1.33	70.93	12378.76	394856.79	39485.68	146.35	8869.74	443.49
23 Mar 2018 15:15	LINGFIELD (A.W)	Roy's Legacy	1	1.58	71.48	22438.68	407235.55	40723.55	261.47	9016.09	450.80
23 Mar 2018 16:00	SEDGEFIELD	Lord Napier	1	1.12	71.60	4898.29	429674.23	42967.42	55.67	9277.56	463.88
23 Mar 2018 16:30	SEDGEFIELD	Kings Eclipse	1	1.45	72.03	18577.98	434572.51	43457.25	210.00	9333.22	466.66
23 Mar 2018 18:15	KEMPTON (A.W)	Ripp Orf	1	1.09	72.11	3874.44	453150.49	45315.05	42.94	9543.22	477.16
23 Mar 2018 20:45	KEMPTON (A.W)	Oregon Gift	1	1.31	72.41	13459.30	457024.93	45702.49	148.59	9586.16	479.31
24 Mar 2018 14:15	BANGOR-ON-DEE	Rons Dream	2	1.74	73.11	33075.05	470484.31	47048.43	360.19	9734.75	486.74

39

THE HORSE RACING PLACE BET INVESTMENT STRATEGY

24 Mar 2018 14:35	LINGFIELD (A.W)	Night Castle	1	1.13	73.23	6218.96	503559.36	50355.94	65.62	10094.93	504.75
24 Mar 2018 14:40	NEWBURY	Oistrakh Le Noir	2	1.23	73.45	11138.66	509778.32	50977.83	116.85	10160.55	508.03
24 Mar 2018 16:20	LINGFIELD (A.W)	Inuk	2	1.59	74.01	29197.40	520916.97	52091.70	303.18	10277.40	513.87
24 Mar 2018 16:55	LINGFIELD (A.W)	Smiley Bagel	3	1.64	74.62	33446.95	550114.37	55011.44	338.58	10580.58	529.03
24 Mar 2018 17:00	NEWBURY	Caribert	1	1.67	75.26	37143.68	583561.32	58356.13	365.79	10919.16	545.96
24 Mar 2018 18:45	WOLVERHAMPTON (	Jazirat	3	1.36	74.26	21228.11	620705.00	62070.50	203.13	11284.95	564.25
25 Mar 2018 14:15	CARLISLE	Our Lucas	1	1.80	75.01	48786.92	641933.11	64193.31	459.52	11488.08	574.40
25 Mar 2018 14:50	CARLISLE	Aye Right	2	1.09	75.10	5905.66	690720.03	69072.00	53.76	11947.60	597.38
25 Mar 2018 15:00	DONCASTER	First Contact	1	1.24	75.33	15883.07	696625.68	69662.57	144.02	12001.37	600.07
26 Mar 2018 13:30	HUNTINGDON	Schiaparannie	3	1.67	75.97	45351.18	712508.75	71250.87	406.87	12145.38	607.27
26 Mar 2018 14:00	HUNTINGDON	Passing Call	2	1.08	76.05	5759.74	757859.93	75785.99	50.21	12552.25	627.61
27 Mar 2018 14:30	SOUTHWELL (A.W)	Kion	3	1.36	75.05	26115.79	763619.67	76361.97	226.84	12602.46	630.12
27 Mar 2018 17:15	HEREFORD	Sackett	1	1.41	75.44	30760.20	789735.46	78973.55	263.00	12829.31	641.47
28 Mar 2018 15:50	WARWICK	Fresh New Dawn	3	1.45	75.87	35076.19	820495.65	82049.57	294.58	13092.31	654.62
28 Mar 2018 16:45	WINCANTON	Unioniste	1	1.16	76.02	13004.69	855571.84	85557.18	107.10	13386.89	669.34
28 Mar 2018 16:55	WARWICK	Now McGinty	1	1.44	76.44	36306.50	868576.54	86857.65	296.87	13493.98	674.70
28 Mar 2018 19:45	NEWCASTLE (A.W)	Fountain Of Time	1	1.15	76.58	12894.58	904883.04	90488.30	103.43	13790.85	689.54
29 Mar 2018 14:00	WETHERBY	Pirate Look	2	1.16	76.73	13950.22	917777.62	91777.76	111.15	13894.28	694.71
29 Mar 2018 14:45	TOWCESTER	Dontminddboys	1	1.63	77.33	55763.91	931727.84	93172.78	441.17	14005.43	700.27
29 Mar 2018 16:05	CHELMSFORD (A.W)	Luna Eclipse	1	1.91	78.19	85368.66	987491.75	98749.17	657.32	14446.61	722.33
29 Mar 2018 16:15	WETHERBY	Bob Mahler	1	1.08	78.27	8153.74	1072860.41	107286.04	60.42	15103.93	755.20
30 Mar 2018 15:40	LINGFIELD (A.W)	Corinthia Knight	1	1.31	78.56	31835.87	1081014.15	108101.42	235.05	15164.34	758.22
31 Mar 2018 14:15	CARLISLE	Elusive Theatre	3	1.33	78.88	34887.85	1112850.02	111285.00	254.09	15399.39	769.97
31 Mar 2018 16:45	MUSSELBURGH	Tommy G	2	1.82	79.66	89408.78	1147737.87	114773.79	641.79	15653.48	782.67
31 Mar 2018 18:45	CHELMSFORD (A.W)	Leoro	2	1.57	80.20	66991.49	1237146.65	123714.66	464.42	16295.27	814.76
01 Apr 2018 14:15	PLUMPTON	Traffic Fluide	1	1.25	80.44	30973.28	1304138.14	130413.81	209.50	16759.69	837.98
01 Apr 2018 16:45	SOUTHWELL (A.W)	Mujassam	1	1.06	80.49	7610.14	1335111.42	133511.14	50.91	16969.18	848.46
01 Apr 2018 16:55	PLUMPTON	The Lion Dancer	1	1.50	80.97	63779.27	1342721.55	134272.16	425.50	17020.09	851.00
01 Apr 2018 17:20	SOUTHWELL (A.W)	Da Capo Dandy	1	1.46	81.41	61464.09	1406500.83	140650.08	401.25	17445.59	872.28
02 Apr 2018 14:00	WOLVERHAMPTON (	Kyllachy Dragon	3	1.60	80.41	83674.00	1467964.91	146796.49	535.41	17846.84	892.34
02 Apr 2018 15:10	WOLVERHAMPTON (	Bartholomeu Dia	1	1.10	80.50	14740.57	1551638.91	155163.89	91.91	18382.25	919.11
03 Apr 2018 15:55	LINGFIELD (A.W)	Ostilio	2	1.14	80.63	20832.85	1566379.48	156637.95	129.32	18474.16	923.71
04 Apr 2018 13:40	LINGFIELD (A.W)	The King's Steed	3	2.02	81.60	153800.87	1587212.33	158721.23	948.78	18603.48	930.17
04 Apr 2018 15:15	LINGFIELD (A.W)	Kalagia	2	2.00	82.55	165396.25	1741013.20	174101.32	977.61	19552.25	977.61
04 Apr 2018 17:15	LINGFIELD (A.W)	Night Story	3	1.48	83.01	86932.27	1906409.46	190640.95	492.72	20529.87	1026.49
04 Apr 2018 18:45	KEMPTON (A.W)	Mordin	1	1.30	83.30	56810.24	1993341.73	199334.17	315.34	21022.58	1051.13
04 Apr 2018 20:15	KEMPTON (A.W)	Exceeding Power	1	2.00	84.25	194764.44	2050151.97	205015.20	1066.90	21337.92	1066.90
04 Apr 2018 20:45	KEMPTON (A.W)	Bird For Life	1	1.37	84.60	78908.81	2244916.40	224491.64	414.49	22404.82	1120.24
05 Apr 2018 17:45	CHELMSFORD (A.W)	Dancing Brave Be	1	1.13	84.73	28699.24	2323825.22	232382.52	148.33	22819.31	1140.97
05 Apr 2018 19:15	CHELMSFORD (A.W)	Tom's Rock	3	1.50	85.20	111744.91	2352524.46	235252.45	574.19	22967.63	1148.38
05 Apr 2018 19:45	CHELMSFORD (A.W)	Poet's Prince	1	1.36	85.54	84278.01	2464269.37	246426.94	423.75	23541.82	1177.09
06 Apr 2018 15:10	FONTWELL	Duke Of Kilcorral	2	1.16	85.69	38737.92	2548547.38	254854.74	191.72	23965.58	1198.28
06 Apr 2018 18:10	CHELMSFORD (A.W)	Miniature Daffod	1	1.49	86.16	120438.13	2587285.30	258728.53	591.85	24157.30	1207.87
06 Apr 2018 18:40	CHELMSFORD (A.W)	Rustang	1	1.63	86.76	162057.25	2707723.43	270772.34	779.60	24749.15	1237.46
07 Apr 2018 15:50	KEMPTON (A.W)	Dathanna	1	1.38	87.12	103599.08	2869780.68	286978.07	485.05	25528.75	1276.44
07 Apr 2018 16:35	FAKENHAM	Step Back	1	1.21	87.32	59318.93	2973379.76	297337.98	273.14	26013.80	1300.69
07 Apr 2018 17:25	UTTOXETER	Rosy World	1	1.72	88.01	207436.59	3032698.69	303269.87	946.33	26286.94	1314.35
07 Apr 2018 17:40	FAKENHAM	Before Midnight	1	1.14	88.14	43093.80	3240135.28	324013.53	190.63	27233.27	1361.66
08 Apr 2018 13:50	CARLISLE	Skywards Reward	1	1.45	88.57	140358.04	3283229.08	328322.91	617.04	27423.91	1371.20
08 Apr 2018 14:05	EXETER	Under The Wood	1	1.09	88.65	29271.67	3423587.12	342358.71	126.18	28040.95	1402.05
08 Apr 2018 17:15	EXETER	Tinkers Hill Tomr	3	1.17	88.81	55763.67	3452858.79	345285.88	239.42	28167.13	1408.36
09 Apr 2018 15:15	WINCANTON	Brynmawr	2	1.75	89.53	249989.35	3508622.46	350862.25	1065.25	28406.55	1420.33
09 Apr 2018 17:45	WOLVERHAMPTON (	Beshaayir	1	1.05	89.58	17853.41	3758611.81	375861.18	73.68	29471.80	1473.59
10 Apr 2018 17:45	WOLVERHAMPTON (	Appenzeller	2	1.33	89.89	118392.18	3776465.22	377646.52	487.50	29545.48	1477.27
10 Apr 2018 18:15	WOLVERHAMPTON (	Ferik	1	1.24	90.11	88802.75	3894857.40	389485.74	360.40	30032.98	1501.65
10 Apr 2018 20:15	WOLVERHAMPTON (	Count Octave	1	1.09	90.20	34060.29	3983660.15	398366.02	136.77	30393.37	1519.67
11 Apr 2018 14:00	MARKET RASEN	Mont Des Avaloi	1	1.06	90.26	22901.01	4017720.44	401772.04	91.59	30530.14	1526.51
11 Apr 2018 15:45	LINGFIELD (A.W)	Geetanjali	3	1.58	89.26	222638.24	4040621.45	404062.15	888.03	30621.73	1531.09
11 Apr 2018 18:15	KEMPTON (A.W)	Magnificent	2	1.43	89.67	174154.16	4263259.69	426325.97	677.46	31509.76	1575.49
11 Apr 2018 18:45	KEMPTON (A.W)	Perfect Hustler	2	1.21	89.87	88526.41	4437413.85	443741.39	337.97	32187.22	1609.36
12 Apr 2018 13:55	SOUTHWELL (A.W)	Gleaming Sun	2	1.32	90.17	137588.58	4525940.26	452594.03	520.40	32525.19	1626.26
12 Apr 2018 14:20	AINTREE	Apple's Shakira	3	1.40	90.55	177214.10	4663528.84	466352.88	660.91	33045.59	1652.28
12 Apr 2018 14:40	TAUNTON	Blu Cavalier	1	1.27	90.81	124165.06	4840742.94	484074.29	455.04	33706.50	1685.33
12 Apr 2018 14:50	AINTREE	Might Bite	1	1.30	91.09	141499.88	4964907.99	496490.80	512.42	34161.54	1708.08
12 Apr 2018 18.45	CHELMSFORD (A.W)	Commander Han	2	1.31	91.39	150383.71	5106407.87	510640.79	537.45	34673.96	1733.70
13 Apr 2018 14:50	AINTREE	Terrefort	1	1.83	92.17	414498.02	5256791.58	525679.16	1461.27	35211.41	1760.57
13 Apr 2018 15:05	SEDGEFIELD	Bulkov	1	1.07	92.24	37714.08	5671289.60	567128.96	128.35	36672.68	1833.63
13 Apr 2018 15:40	SEDGEFIELD	Frankie Ballou	1	1.48	92.70	260330.57	5709003.68	570900.37	883.22	36801.04	1840.05
13 Apr 2018 16:15	SEDGEFIELD	Knockrobin	2	1.13	92.82	73721.28	5969334.24	596933.42	244.95	37684.26	1884.21
13 Apr 2018 20:15	KEMPTON (A.W)	Casima	1	1.71	93.49	407604.09	6043055.52	604305.55	1346.49	37929.21	1896.46
14 Apr 2018 14:30	LINGFIELD (A.W)	Betty F	3	1.28	93.76	171587.55	6450659.62	645065.96	549.86	39275.70	1963.78
14 Apr 2018 15:55	NEWCASTLE	Grand Morning	1	1.99	94.70	622822.35	6622247.16	662224.72	1971.37	39825.56	1991.28
14 Apr 2018 16:05	CHEPSTOW	Kimberlite Candy	1	2.30	95.93	894766.08	7245069.51	724506.95	2716.80	41796.92	2089.85
14 Apr 2018 16:15	LINGFIELD (A.W)	Dorian Gray	2	1.34	96.25	262916.69	8139835.59	813983.56	756.73	44513.72	2225.69
14 Apr 2018 18:30	WOLVERHAMPTON (	Avocet	3	1.58	96.81	462991.65	8402752.28	840275.23	1312.84	45270.46	2263.52
15 Apr 2018 16:20	FFOS LAS	Royal Claret	3	2.14	97.89	960160.07	8865743.93	886574.39	2655.25	46583.30	2329.16
15 Apr 2018 17:20	FFOS LAS	Smiths Cross	2	1.43	98.30	401388.18	9825904.00	982590.40	1058.63	49238.55	2461.93
15 Apr 2018 17:30	PLUMPTON	Baddesley Knight	1	1.45	98.72	437216.74	10227292.18	1022729.22	1131.69	50297.18	2514.86
17 Apr 2018 14:00	EXETER	Master Tommytu	1	1.12	98.84	121575.40	10664508.92	1066450.89	308.57	51428.86	2571.44
17 Apr 2018 16:30	CARLISLE	Skywards Reward	1	1.10	98.93	102467.80	10786084.32	1078608.43	258.69	51737.44	2586.87
17 Apr 2018 16:45	NEWMARKET	Kew Gardens	3	1.43	99.34	444797.35	10888552.12	1088855.21	1117.92	51996.12	2599.81
18 Apr 2018 17:45	KEMPTON (A.W)	Jungle Inthebung	2	1.50	99.82	538334.10	11333349.48	1133334.95	1327.85	53114.04	2655.70
19 Apr 2018 16:45	NEWMARKET	Argentello	3	1.37	100.16	417289.68	11871683.58	1187168.36	1007.17	54441.89	2722.09
19 Apr 2018 20:45	NEWCASTLE (A.W)	Emaraaty	1	1.09	100.25	105070.72	12288973.25	1228897.33	249.52	55449.06	2772.45
20 Apr 2018 17:10	BATH	Kinks	1	1.25	100.48	294358.54	12394043.98	1239404.40	696.23	55698.59	2784.93
20 Apr 2018 17:15	AYR	Bob Mahler	2	2.46	101.87	1759881.43	12688402.52	1268840.25	4116.82	56394.82	2819.74
20 Apr 2018 18:45	BATH	Cowboy Soldier	2	1.18	102.04	247065.66	14448283.95	1444828.40	544.60	60511.64	3025.58
21 Apr 2018 13:55	THIRSK	Wasntexpectingt	2	1.14	102.17	195448.15	14695349.61	1469534.96	427.39	61056.24	3052.81
21 Apr 2018 16:15	THIRSK	Tuff Rock	2	1.87	103.00	1230724.43	14890797.76	1489079.78	2674.54	61483.64	3074.18

THE HORSE RACING PLACE BET INVESTMENT STRATEGY

22 Apr 2018 14:15	WINCANTON	Blu Cavalier	1	1.21	103.20	321624.37	16121522.19	1612152.22	673.66	64158.18	3207.91
22 Apr 2018 15:30	MARKET RASEN	One Style	1	1.90	104.05	1405889.03	16443146.56	1644314.66	2917.43	64831.84	3241.59
22 Apr 2018 16:25	WINCANTON	Diamond Guy	1	1.54	104.57	915655.53	17849035.59	1784903.56	1829.23	67749.27	3387.46
22 Apr 2018 16:35	MARKET RASEN	Otter Moon	1	1.74	105.27	1319157.79	18764691.11	1876469.11	2574.40	69578.50	3478.93
22 Apr 2018 17:05	MARKET RASEN	Wolf Sword	1	1.90	106.12	1717169.08	20083848.90	2008384.89	3246.88	72152.90	3607.65
22 Apr 2018 17:40	MARKET RASEN	Legal Eyes	2	2.02	107.09	2112518.64	21801017.98	2180101.80	3845.39	75399.79	3769.99
23 Apr 2018 13:50	HEXHAM	Whoshotwho	2	1.15	107.24	340767.90	23913536.62	2391353.66	594.34	79245.17	3962.26
23 Apr 2018 14:00	NEWTON ABBOT	Sensulano	2	1.22	107.45	506914.96	24254304.52	2425430.45	878.23	79839.51	3991.98
23 Apr 2018 14:10	PONTEFRACT	Carey Street	1	1.73	108.15	1717190.57	24761219.48	2476121.95	2946.20	80717.75	4035.89
23 Apr 2018 14:50	HEXHAM	Pineapple Rush	1	1.19	108.33	477935.30	26478410.06	2647841.01	794.81	83663.95	4183.20
23 Apr 2018 16:55	HEXHAM	Mendip Express	1	1.30	108.61	768255.84	26956345.36	2695634.54	1266.88	84458.75	4222.94
23 Apr 2018 18:50	WINDSOR	Fajjaj	2	1.61	109.18	1606640.64	27724601.20	2772460.12	2614.63	85725.63	4286.28
24 Apr 2018 13:50	YARMOUTH	Luchador	3	1.30	109.47	835940.39	29331241.84	2933124.18	1325.10	88340.27	4417.01
24 Apr 2018 14:00	LUDLOW	Gumball	1	1.07	109.53	200611.76	30167182.23	3016718.22	313.83	89665.37	4483.27
24 Apr 2018 14:15	EXETER	Point N Shoot	1	1.30	109.82	865482.13	30367793.99	3036779.40	1349.69	89979.20	4498.96
24 Apr 2018 14:55	YARMOUTH	Without Parole	1	1.13	109.95	385730.96	31233276.12	3123327.61	593.64	91328.89	4566.44
24 Apr 2018 16:30	YARMOUTH	Oud Metha Bridg	3	1.49	110.41	1471864.78	31619007.08	3161900.71	2252.10	91922.53	4596.13
24 Apr 2018 16:35	HUNTINGDON	Eskendash	3	1.13	110.54	408672.27	33090871.86	3309087.19	612.14	94174.63	4708.73
24 Apr 2018 17:15	LUDLOW	Imperial Aura	1	1.20	110.72	636491.34	33499544.13	3349954.41	947.87	94786.76	4739.34
24 Apr 2018 17:35	EXETER	Master Baker	2	1.44	111.14	1426886.28	34136035.47	3413603.55	2106.16	95734.63	4786.73
25 Apr 2018 14:45	EPSOM	Dee Ex Bee	3	1.47	111.59	1507004.40	35562921.75	3556292.17	2299.26	97840.79	4892.04
25 Apr 2018 15:45	PERTH	The Jam Man	3	1.67	112.22	2364648.82	37150806.21	3715080.62	3354.69	100140.05	5007.00
25 Apr 2018 16:25	EPSOM	King Of The Sand	3	1.27	112.48	1013571.42	39515455.02	3951545.50	1397.18	103494.74	5174.74
25 Apr 2018 16:45	PERTH	Morning With Iva	1	1.78	113.23	3003200.86	40529026.44	4052902.64	4090.78	104891.92	5244.60
25 Apr 2018 16:50	LINGFIELD (A.W)	No More Thrills	1	1.74	113.94	3060315.58	43532227.30	4353222.73	4032.36	108982.71	5449.14
25 Apr 2018 17:15	TAUNTON	Cockney Wren	1	1.24	114.16	1062309.98	46592542.88	4659254.29	1356.18	113015.07	5650.75
25 Apr 2018 17:20	LINGFIELD (A.W)	Black Sails	1	1.15	114.31	679081.65	47654852.86	4765485.29	857.78	114371.25	5718.56
25 Apr 2018 17:45	TAUNTON	Don't Ask	1	1.20	114.50	918344.76	48333934.51	4833393.45	1152.29	115229.03	5761.45
25 Apr 2018 18:25	LINGFIELD (A.W)	Caspar The Cub	2	1.15	114.64	701844.98	49252279.27	4925227.93	872.86	116381.32	5819.07
26 Apr 2018 13:50	PERTH	Cornerstone Lad	3	1.17	114.80	806759.11	49954124.25	4995412.42	996.66	117254.18	5862.71
26 Apr 2018 20:35	CHELMSFORD (A.W)	Luna Eclipse	1	[illegible]	115.40	3327375.90	50760883.35	5076088.34	4079.65	118250.84	5912.54
27 Apr 2018 14:25	SANDOWN	Crystal Ocean	1	1.47	115.91	2415040.78	54088259.26	5408825.93	2874.77	122330.50	6116.52
27 Apr 2018 15:00	SANDOWN	Sevenna Star	1	1.39	116.28	2093447.27	56503300.03	5650330.00	2441.50	125205.26	6260.26
27 Apr 2018 16:05	SANDOWN	Diamond Dougal	2	1.38	116.64	2115342.58	58596747.30	5859674.73	2425.29	127646.77	6382.34
27 Apr 2018 16:45	PERTH	Cultram Abbey	1	1.14	116.77	807470.80	60712089.88	6071208.99	910.50	130072.05	6503.60
27 Apr 2018 18:50	TOWCESTER	Transpennine Sta	2	1.37	117.12	2162412.56	61519560.67	6151956.07	2423.18	130982.56	6549.13
27 Apr 2018 19:00	CHEPSTOW	Tinkers Hill Tomr	1	1.35	117.45	2117425.61	63681973.23	6368197.32	2334.60	133405.74	6670.29
27 Apr 2018 19:20	TOWCESTER	Fight Commande	2	1.19	117.63	1187679.15	65799398.84	6579939.88	1289.53	135740.34	6787.02
27 Apr 2018 19:55	TOWCESTER	Miss Heritage	2	1.71	118.30	4518278.41	66987077.99	6698707.80	4864.56	137029.87	6851.49
28 Apr 2018 15:00	SANDOWN	Altior	1	1.14	118.44	951021.24	71505356.40	7150535.64	993.26	141894.43	7094.72
28 Apr 2018 18:15	DONCASTER	Ornamental	1	1.21	118.64	1445504.73	72456377.64	7245637.76	1500.32	142887.69	7144.38
28 Apr 2018 19:00	WOLVERHAMPTON	Glencadam Glory	1	1.06	118.70	421240.73	73901882.37	7390188.24	433.16	144388.01	7219.40
29 Apr 2018 14:10	WETHERBY	Regulator	3	1.42	119.10	2965492.61	74323123.10	7432312.31	3041.24	144821.17	7241.06
29 Apr 2018 15:40	SALISBURY	Billy Ray	1	1.89	119.94	6534752.46	77288615.72	7728861.57	6579.88	147862.42	7393.12
29 Apr 2018 16:45	SALISBURY	Foxtrot Lady	2	2.24	121.12	9874392.77	83823368.17	8382336.82	9575.42	154442.30	7722.11
30 Apr 2018 15:15	WOLVERHAMPTON	Tivoli	1	1.38	121.48	3382489.17	93697760.94	9369776.09	3116.34	164017.72	8200.89
30 Apr 2018 16:15	SALISBURY	Seasearch	2	1.11	121.58	1014488.61	97080250.11	9708025.01	919.24	167134.06	8356.70
30 Apr 2018 17:05	THIRSK	Odds On Oli	1	2.15	122.68	10716850.21	98094738.73	9809473.87	9663.06	168053.29	8402.66
30 Apr 2018 17:40	WINDSOR	Blown By Wind	2	1.16	122.83	1653936.15	108811588.93	10881158.89	1421.73	177716.36	8885.82
30 Apr 2018 17:50	SOUTHWELL (A.W)	Mr Buttons	2	1.20	123.02	2098844.98	110465525.09	11046552.51	1791.38	179138.09	8956.90
01 May 2018 14:30	NOTTINGHAM	Mushtaq	3	1.68	123.67	7271658.31	112564370.06	11256437.01	6151.60	180929.47	9046.47
01 May 2018 15:35	NOTTINGHAM	Red Tea	1	1.75	124.38	8538317.02	119836028.37	11983602.84	7015.54	187081.07	9354.05
01 May 2018 15:55	BRIGHTON	Precious Ramotsi	1	1.84	125.18	10244272.76	128374345.39	12837434.54	8152.06	194096.61	9704.83
01 May 2018 17:45	KEMPTON (A.W)	Its The Only Way	1	1.25	125.41	3292192.18	138618618.15	13861861.82	2528.11	202248.67	10112.43
01 May 2018 18:15	KEMPTON (A.W)	Chynna	3	1.39	125.78	5257795.52	141910810.33	14191081.03	3993.15	204776.78	10238.84
01 May 2018 18:25	NEWCASTLE (A.W)	Walk On Walter	1	1.45	126.21	6291457.90	147168605.86	14716860.59	4697.32	208769.93	10438.50
02 May 2018 14:35	ASCOT	Dathanna	1	1.09	126.30	1312083.55	153460063.76	15346006.38	960.60	213467.25	10673.36
02 May 2018 15:45	ASCOT	Invincible Army	1	1.34	126.62	4999140.36	154772147.30	15477214.73	3645.27	214427.85	10721.39
02 May 2018 17:00	BRIGHTON	Tin Hat	1	1.07	126.69	1062479.06	159771287.66	15977128.77	763.26	218073.12	10903.66
02 May 2018 17:40	PONTEFRACT	Foxtrot Knight	1	1.41	127.08	6264475.21	160833766.72	16083376.67	4486.15	218836.38	10941.82
03 May 2018 15:10	REDCAR	Robsdelight	1	1.24	127.31	3809839.92	167098241.94	16709824.19	2679.87	223322.53	11166.13
03 May 2018 15:20	SOUTHWELL (A.W)	Victory Wave	2	1.09	127.39	1461264.10	170908081.85	17090808.19	1017.01	226002.40	11300.12
03 May 2018 15:30	LINGFIELD (A.W)	Captain Lars	1	[illegible]	127.43	982505.27	172369345.95	17236934.60	681.06	227019.41	11350.97
03 May 2018 18:40	MUSSELBURGH	Soldier's Minute	3	1.07	126.45	1152789.81	173351851.22	17335185.12	796.95	227700.47	11385.02
03 May 2018 19:10	MUSSELBURGH	Northwest Fronti	3	1.28	126.72	4641823.45	174504641.04	17450464.10	3198.96	228497.42	11424.87
03 May 2018 19:40	MUSSELBURGH	Been The Lyte	1	1.49	127.19	8339267.92	179146464.49	17914646.45	5676.56	231696.38	11584.82
04 May 2018 14:30	CHEPSTOW	King Lud	2	1.22	127.39	3918451.81	187485732.41	18748573.24	2611.10	237372.94	11868.65
04 May 2018 16:40	MUSSELBURGH	Trading Point	1	1.22	127.60	4000347.45	191404184.22	19140418.42	2639.83	239984.04	11999.20
05 May 2018 15:20	UTTOXETER	Bags Groove	3	1.55	128.10	9838618.17	195404531.67	19540453.17	6429.53	242623.87	12131.19
05 May 2018 16:25	GOODWOOD	Qaroun	1	1.77	128.83	15013536.41	205243149.84	20524314.98	9588.56	249053.40	12452.67
05 May 2018 16:55	WETHERBY	Saroog	2	1.09	128.92	1883194.67	220256686.25	22025668.62	1163.89	258641.96	12932.10
05 May 2018 17:00	GOODWOOD	Honey Man	3	1.44	129.34	9285447.02	222139880.91	22213988.09	5715.73	259805.85	12990.29
06 May 2018 13:00	TOWCESTER	French Crusader	1	1.18	129.51	3957373.11	231425327.94	23142532.79	2389.69	265521.58	13276.08
06 May 2018 14:05	HAMILTON	Bengali Boys	3	1.47	128.51	10509837.60	235382701.04	23538270.10	6295.91	267911.27	13395.56
06 May 2018 15:15	TOWCESTER	Doux Pretender	1	1.13	128.63	3036772.85	245892538.64	24589253.86	1782.35	274207.18	13710.36
06 May 2018 16:45	NEWMARKET	Lah Ti Dar	1	1.54	129.14	12770073.68	248929311.50	24892931.15	7451.72	275989.53	13799.48
07 May 2018 14:45	AYR	Return Ticket	1	1.22	129.35	5469517.15	261699385.18	26169938.52	3117.85	283441.25	14172.06
07 May 2018 15:55	AYR	Clondaw Kaempf	2	1.13	129.48	3299535.94	267168902.33	26716890.23	1862.63	286559.10	14327.96
07 May 2018 17:25	BEVERLEY	Expensive Liaison	1	1.19	129.66	4881955.31	270468438.27	27046843.83	2740.01	288421.74	14421.09
07 May 2018 17:30	WARWICK	Hollow Park	2	1.57	130.20	14910223.81	275350393.58	27535039.36	8298.11	291161.74	14558.09
07 May 2018 18:10	AYR	Glinger Flame	3	1.41	130.59	11305651.05	290260617.39	29026061.74	6138.93	299459.85	14972.99
08 May 2018 14:10	FAKENHAM	Ascendant	1	1.19	130.77	5443271.15	301566268.44	30156626.84	2903.19	305598.78	15279.94
08 May 2018 14:30	BRIGHTON	Haylah	2	1.45	131.20	13124657.82	307009539.59	30700953.96	6941.29	308501.97	15425.10
08 May 2018 14:50	THIRSK	Feathery	1	1.42	131.60	12773354.48	320134197.40	32013419.74	6624.31	315443.26	15772.16
08 May 2018 16:25	THIRSK	Militia	1	1.12	131.71	3796140.09	332907551.88	33290755.19	1932.41	322067.57	16103.38
08 May 2018 17:25	THIRSK	Vive La Differenc	2	1.57	132.25	18232451.10	336702697.97	33670269.80	9234.00	323999.98	16200.00
08 May 2018 17:30	LUDLOW	Diamond Guy	1	1.06	132.31	2023130.35	354935149.07	35493514.91	999.70	333233.98	16661.70
09 May 2018 14:00	KELSO	Calix Delafayette	3	1.14	132.44	4747545.12	356958279.42	35695827.94	2339.64	334233.68	16711.68
09 May 2018 16:05	CHESTER	Argentello	3	1.27	132.70	9277754.40	361705824.53	36170582.45	4543.74	336573.31	16828.67

THE HORSE RACING PLACE BET INVESTMENT STRATEGY

09 May 2018 17:15	KELSO	Akarita Lights	1	1.35	133.03	12335204.00	370983578.93	37098357.89	5969.55	341117.05	17055.85
10 May 2018 15:20	WORCESTER	Rock Of Leon	1	1.33	133.34	12017043.84	383318782.93	38331878.29	5726.93	347086.60	17354.33
10 May 2018 15:35	CHESTER	Idaho	1	1.35	133.68	13144916.24	395335826.78	39533582.68	6174.24	352813.53	17640.68
10 May 2018 16:05	CHESTER	Ynys Mon	2	1.27	133.94	10477531.06	408480743.02	40848074.30	4846.33	358987.77	17949.39
10 May 2018 16:35	CHESTER	Ghostwatch	3	1.48	134.40	19104497.30	418958274.08	41895827.41	8732.02	363834.10	18191.71
10 May 2018 17:20	WINCANTON	Ringa Ding Ding	2	1.14	134.53	5826234.86	438062771.37	43806277.14	2607.96	372566.12	18628.31
10 May 2018 18:50	WINCANTON	Orbasa	3	1.57	135.07	24036589.69	443889006.23	44388900.62	10692.46	375174.08	18758.70
10 May 2018 20:40	CHELMSFORD (A.W)	Elgin	1	1.05	135.12	2222646.58	467925595.92	46792559.59	964.67	385866.54	19293.33
11 May 2018 14:50	LINGFIELD	Glory Fighter	1	1.13	135.24	5806330.79	470148242.50	47014824.25	2514.40	386831.21	19341.56
11 May 2018 16:05	CHESTER	Kachy	1	1.25	135.48	11303921.12	475954573.30	47595457.33	4866.82	389345.61	19467.28
11 May 2018 17:40	NOTTINGHAM	Raa Atoll	1	1.18	135.65	8332120.25	487258494.41	48725849.44	3547.91	394212.43	19710.62
12 May 2018 13:45	HEXHAM	Birch Vale	1	1.12	135.77	5649733.01	495590614.67	49559061.47	2386.56	397760.35	19888.02
12 May 2018 14:05	NOTTINGHAM	Tabdeed	1	1.29	136.04	13809171.58	501240347.67	50124034.77	5802.13	400146.91	20007.35
12 May 2018 14:15	ASCOT	Count Calabash	1	2.06	137.05	51865486.59	515049519.25	51504951.93	21515.30	405949.04	20297.45
12 May 2018 15:50	NOTTINGHAM	Pretty Baby	1	1.29	137.32	15618508.41	566915005.84	56691500.58	6198.23	427464.34	21373.22
12 May 2018 17:50	LINGFIELD	Whitefountainfai	1	1.32	137.63	17709018.83	582533514.25	58253351.43	6938.60	433662.57	21683.13
12 May 2018 18:00	WARWICK	Deyrann De Carja	1	1.13	137.76	7412995.28	600242533.08	60024253.31	2863.91	440601.17	22030.06
12 May 2018 18:45	THIRSK	Stonific	1	1.81	138.53	46759092.91	607655528.37	60765552.84	17960.34	443465.08	22173.25
14 May 2018 15:15	KEMPTON	Bandsman	1	1.41	138.92	25489449.50	654414621.28	65441462.13	9459.22	461425.41	23071.27
14 May 2018 17:30	TOWCESTER	Misty Bloom	2	1.63	139.52	40692258.64	679904070.77	67990407.08	14832.87	470884.64	23544.23
14 May 2018 18:30	TOWCESTER	Nikki Steel	2	1.25	139.76	17114162.82	720596329.41	72059632.94	6071.47	485717.50	24285.88
14 May 2018 20:00	TOWCESTER	Royalraise	1	1.38	140.12	26631348.77	737710492.23	73771049.22	9343.99	491788.97	24589.45
15 May 2018 14:20	WINCANTON	The Detainee	3	1.54	139.12	39210736.44	764341841.00	76434184.10	13530.59	501132.96	25056.65
15 May 2018 15:30	SEDGEFIELD	Curious Carlos	1	1.20	139.30	15267498.97	803552577.45	80355257.74	5146.64	514663.55	25733.18
15 May 2018 16:30	SEDGEFIELD	General Mahler	3	1.39	138.30	30337283.83	818820076.42	81882007.64	10136.30	519810.19	25990.51
15 May 2018 17:20	WINCANTON	Unioniste	2	1.13	138.42	10487093.40	849157360.25	84915736.02	3444.65	529946.48	26497.32
15 May 2018 17:45	BEVERLEY	Georgian Manor	1	1.10	138.52	8166622.31	859644453.65	85964445.36	2666.96	533391.14	26669.56
15 May 2018 19:30	SOUTHWELL	Settie Hill	1	1.04	138.56	3297682.09	867811075.96	86781107.60	1072.12	536058.09	26802.90
16 May 2018 14:00	NEWTON ABBOT	King Calvin	1	1.17	138.72	14068406.44	871108758.05	87110875.80	4565.61	537130.21	26856.51
16 May 2018 15:10	NEWTON ABBOT	Oskar Denarius	1	1.38	139.08	31954895.64	885177164.49	88517716.45	10292.22	541695.82	27084.79
16 May 2018 15:20	YARMOUTH	Raven Banner	2	1.32	139.39	27880814.63	917132060.13	91713206.01	8831.81	551988.04	27599.40
16 May 2018 15:30	YORK	Harry Angel	1	1.20	139.57	17955244.62	945012874.76	94501287.48	5608.20	560819.84	28040.99
16 May 2018 17:05	YORK	World Order	2	1.31	139.87	28359411.12	962968119.38	96296811.94	8779.63	566428.04	28321.40
16 May 2018 18:05	PERTH	Champ	1	1.04	139.90	3767044.62	991327530.49	99132753.05	1150.42	575207.68	28760.38
16 May 2018 18:55	BATH	Francophilia	2	1.28	140.17	26469515.70	995094575.11	99509457.51	8069.01	576358.09	28817.90
16 May 2018 20:05	PERTH	Shanaway	2	2.18	141.29	114517334.58	1021564090.80	102156409.08	34481.20	584427.11	29221.36
16 May 2018 20:25	BATH	Christmas Night	2	1.35	141.63	37774707.39	1136081425.38	113608142.54	10830.90	618908.31	30945.42
16 May 2018 21:05	PERTH	Creevytennant	1	1.30	141.91	33454899.78	1173856132.78	117385613.28	9446.09	629739.20	31486.96
17 May 2018 14:00	PERTH	Subcontinent	1	1.13	142.03	14910291.25	1207311032.56	120731103.26	4154.70	639185.29	31959.26
17 May 2018 16:15	PERTH	Morning With Iva	1	1.64	142.64	74311056.49	1222221323.81	122222132.38	20586.88	643339.99	32167.00
17 May 2018 17:45	NEWMARKET	Usain Boat	1	1.44	143.06	54195053.50	1296532380.30	129653238.03	14606.39	663926.87	33196.34
17 May 2018 18:20	NEWMARKET	Ziarah	2	1.61	143.64	78274654.79	1350727433.80	135072743.38	20695.26	678533.26	33926.66
17 May 2018 18:40	FONTWELL	Monsieur Gibralt	1	1.15	143.79	20363279.76	1429002088.59	142900208.86	5244.21	699228.53	34961.43
17 May 2018 19:30	NEWMARKET	Stylehunter	2	1.54	144.30	74352443.40	1449365368.35	144936536.84	19020.76	704472.74	35223.64
18 May 2018 14:10	NEWMARKET	Warsaan	1	1.42	144.70	60796340.69	1523717811.75	152371781.17	15193.36	723493.51	36174.68
18 May 2018 15:30	YORK	Stradivarius	1	1.18	144.87	27095192.01	1584514152.44	158451415.24	6648.18	738686.87	36934.34
18 May 2018 15:40	NEWBURY	Nordic Passage	2	1.36	145.22	55117039.58	1611609344.44	161160934.44	13416.03	745335.05	37266.75
18 May 2018 16:25	NEWMARKET	Herculean	2	1.25	145.46	39584751.62	1666726384.02	166672638.40	9484.39	758751.08	37937.55
18 May 2018 16:45	NEWBURY	King's Proctor	2	1.53	145.96	85912765.68	1706311135.64	170631113.56	20358.24	768235.47	38411.77
18 May 2018 19:10	AINTREE	Not That Fuisse	1	1.07	146.03	11918288.94	1792223901.32	179222390.13	2760.08	788593.71	39429.69
19 May 2018 14:10	THIRSK	Queen Of Bermu	1	1.11	146.13	18853285.89	1804142190.27	180414219.03	4352.45	791353.79	39567.69
19 May 2018 14:25	NEWBURY	Crystal Ocean	1	1.14	146.26	24245839.83	1822995476.15	182299547.62	5569.94	795706.24	39785.31
19 May 2018 17:25	NEWBURY	Ripp Orf	2	1.46	146.70	80724445.51	1847241315.99	184724131.60	18429.35	801276.18	40063.81
19 May 2018 17:40	THIRSK	Celestial Force	1	1.40	147.08	73262698.94	1927965761.50	192796576.15	16394.11	819705.53	40985.28
19 May 2018 18:05	UTTOXETER	Just A Feeling	1	1.34	147.40	64639679.27	2001228460.43	200122846.04	14213.69	836099.64	41804.98
19 May 2018 18:20	DONCASTER	Victory Comman	1	2.00	148.35	196257473.27	2065868139.70	206586813.97	42515.67	850313.34	42515.67
20 May 2018 14:00	STRATFORD	Henry's Joy	2	1.23	148.58	49427444.64	2262125612.98	226212561.30	10267.53	892829.00	44641.45
20 May 2018 14:10	MARKET RASEN	L'Inganno Felice	1	1.31	148.87	68075237.55	2311553057.62	231155305.76	13998.00	903096.54	45154.83
20 May 2018 15:20	MARKET RASEN	Elkstone	2	1.38	149.23	85904581.46	2379628295.17	237962829.52	17424.80	917094.53	45854.73
20 May 2018 15:40	STRATFORD	Fingerontheswit	3	1.29	149.51	67925430.75	2465532876.62	246553287.66	13550.53	934519.33	46725.97
20 May 2018 16:00	RIPON	Magical Dreamer	2	1.98	150.44	235864968.42	2533458307.37	253345830.74	46455.42	948069.86	47403.49
20 May 2018 16:30	RIPON	Tigre Du Terre	1	1.01	150.45	2630857.11	2769323275.79	276932327.58	497.26	994525.28	49726.26
20 May 2018 17:25	MARKET RASEN	Forgot To Ask	1	1.37	150.80	97434187.77	2771954132.90	277195413.29	18407.92	995022.54	49751.13
21 May 2018 14:05	REDCAR	Big Ace	2	1.34	151.12	92681242.76	2869388320.67	286938832.07	17228.32	1013430.46	50671.52
21 May 2018 14:55	TOWCESTER	Windspiel	1	1.74	151.83	208233490.31	2962069563.43	296206956.34	38134.37	1030658.78	51532.94
21 May 2018 19:00	LEICESTER	Making Miracles	1	1.16	151.98	48188606.42	3170303053.74	317030305.37	8550.35	1068793.15	53439.66
21 May 2018 19:45	WINDSOR	The Tin Man	1	1.78	152.72	238490232.02	3218491660.16	321849166.02	42016.40	1077343.50	53867.17
22 May 2018 14:55	NOTTINGHAM	Austin Powers	3	1.22	152.93	72250921.55	3456981892.17	345698189.22	12312.96	1119359.90	55967.99
22 May 2018 16:10	AYR	Masham Star	2	1.43	153.34	144169160.44	3529232813.72	352923281.37	24330.97	1131672.85	56583.64
22 May 2018 18:30	HEXHAM	Sleep In First	1	1.47	153.79	164017398.15	3673401974.16	367340197.42	27166.09	1156003.82	57800.19
22 May 2018 18:40	HUNTINGDON	Robert's Star	1	1.31	154.08	113012000.51	3837419372.31	383741937.23	18339.13	1183169.91	59158.50
22 May 2018 20:00	HEXHAM	Card Game	3	1.75	153.08	281468235.31	3950431372.82	395043137.28	45056.59	1201509.04	60075.45
23 May 2018 14:00	AYR	Two Blondes	3	1.32	152.08	128649748.09	4231899608.14	423189960.81	19945.05	1246565.63	62328.28
23 May 2018 14:40	WARWICK	Black Sam Bella	1	1.43	152.49	178128441.20	4360549356.22	436054935.62	27229.98	1266510.68	63325.53
23 May 2018 18:25	KEMPTON (A.W)	Jawwaal	1	1.10	152.59	43117439.08	4538677797.42	453867779.74	6468.70	1293740.66	64687.03
24 May 2018 13:30	GOODWOOD	Mutawaffer	1	1.30	152.87	130581164.24	4581795236.50	458179523.65	19503.14	1300209.37	65010.47
24 May 2018 13:50	CATTERICK	Diviner	3	1.19	153.06	85058394.03	4712376400.74	471237640.07	12537.27	1319712.51	65985.63
24 May 2018 20:20	CHELMSFORD (A.W)	Yeah Baby Yeah	1	1.70	153.72	319029413.85	4797434794.77	479743479.48	46628.74	1332249.78	66612.49
25 May 2018 14:00	GOODWOOD	Big Boots	2	1.35	154.05	170122434.94	5116464208.63	511646420.86	24130.37	1378878.52	68943.93
25 May 2018 14:45	BATH	New Queen	3	1.27	153.05	135600947.41	5286586643.56	528658664.36	18940.62	1403008.89	70150.44
25 May 2018 15:20	BATH	Juneau	1	1.20	153.24	103021564.23	5422187590.97	542218759.10	14219.50	1421949.51	71097.48
25 May 2018 15:30	HAYDOCK	Shepherd Marke	2	1.36	153.59	188962153.11	5525209155.20	552520915.52	25851.04	1436169.01	71808.45
25 May 2018 16:20	GOODWOOD	George Bowen	2	1.82	154.37	445133944.92	5714171308.31	571417130.83	59942.82	1462020.05	73101.00
25 May 2018 17:45	HAYDOCK	Spice War	3	1.74	155.07	432999159.30	6159305253.22	615930525.32	56312.63	1521962.07	76098.14
25 May 2018 18:15	WORCESTER	Robin The Raven	3	1.23	154.07	144041851.41	6592304412.52	659230441.25	18150.17	1578275.50	78913.77
25 May 2018 19:45	WORCESTER	The Bottom Bar	2	1.10	154.16	63995289.51	6736346263.94	673634626.39	7982.13	1596425.67	79821.28
25 May 2018 20:45	WORCESTER	Marvellous Mont	3	1.60	154.73	387619468.55	6800341553.45	680034155.34	48132.23	1604407.79	80220.39
26 May 2018 15:45	GOODWOOD	Mirage Dancer	1	1.35	155.06	238999703.98	7187961021.99	718796102.20	28919.45	1652540.03	82627.00
26 May 2018 15:50	CARTMEL	Jeannot De Nona	1	1.11	155.16	77611739.59	7426960725.97	742696072.60	9248.03	1681459.48	84072.97

THE HORSE RACING PLACE BET INVESTMENT STRATEGY

26 May 2018 16:05	CHESTER	Vange	1	1.48	155.62	342208504.43	7504572465.56	750457246.56	40576.98	1690707.51	84535.38
26 May 2018 16:15	YORK	I Am A Dreamer	1	1.64	156.23	477084282.98	7846780969.99	784678097.00	55401.10	1731284.49	86564.22
26 May 2018 16:35	HAYDOCK	Different League	3	1.89	157.08	703782807.14	8323865252.96	832386525.30	79507.51	1786685.59	89334.28
26 May 2018 17:50	SALISBURY	Well Done Fox	1	1.05	157.12	42881328.29	9027648060.10	902764806.01	4665.48	1866193.10	93309.65
26 May 2018 18:05	FFOS LAS	Francky Du Berla	1	1.44	157.54	379148128.43	9070529388.39	907052938.84	41158.89	1870858.58	93542.93
26 May 2018 21:05	FFOS LAS	Court Royale	3	1.58	158.09	520677231.18	9449677516.82	944967751.68	55448.51	1912017.47	95600.87
28 May 2018 13:30	HUNTINGDON	Fifty Shades	2	1.27	158.35	255739599.29	9970354748.00	997035474.80	26560.79	1967465.98	98373.30
28 May 2018 13:50	REDCAR	The Great Heir	1	1.49	158.82	476024691.87	10226094347.29	1022609434.73	48853.66	1994026.77	99701.34
28 May 2018 14:05	CHELMSFORD (A.W)	The Last Party	1	1.33	159.13	335511431.88	10702119039.15	1070211903.92	33707.53	2042880.42	102144.02
28 May 2018 15:20	CARTMEL	Souriyan	3	1.65	159.75	681573681.59	11037630471.03	1103763047.10	67489.11	2076587.95	103829.40
28 May 2018 16:25	CHELMSFORD (A.W)	Precious Silk	1	1.76	160.47	846126539.82	11719204152.62	1171920415.26	81474.93	2144077.06	107203.85
28 May 2018 16:45	REDCAR	Scottish Summit	2	1.49	160.93	584916143.73	12565330692.43	1256533069.24	54526.02	2225551.99	111277.60
28 May 2018 17:15	LEICESTER	Amuletum	1	1.16	161.08	199883751.91	13150246836.17	1315024683.62	18240.62	2280078.01	114003.90
28 May 2018 17:25	WINDSOR	Mordin	2	1.63	161.67	799005315.70	13350130588.08	1335013058.81	72397.04	2298318.63	114915.93
29 May 2018 15:30	REDCAR	Worth Waiting	1	1.12	161.79	161300149.30	14149135903.77	1414913590.38	14224.29	2370715.67	118535.78
29 May 2018 15:40	LINGFIELD (A.W)	Sawwaah	2	1.21	161.99	285493199.26	14310436053.08	1431043605.31	25041.87	2384939.97	119247.00
29 May 2018 15:50	LEICESTER	Fanaar	1	1.23	162.21	318921054.16	14595929252.34	1459592925.23	27714.79	2409981.84	120499.09
29 May 2018 16:00	REDCAR	Carlton Frankie	1	1.44	162.63	623440742.81	14914850306.50	1491485030.65	53629.33	2437696.63	121884.83
29 May 2018 17:00	REDCAR	Rickyroadboy	1	1.84	163.42	1239955625.74	15538291049.31	1553829104.93	104635.69	2491325.95	124566.30
29 May 2018 19:40	WOLVERHAMPTON	Ledham	1	1.15	163.57	239090015.12	16778246675.05	1677824667.50	19469.71	2595961.64	129798.08
30 May 2018 14:40	CARTMEL	Russian Royale	2	1.94	164.46	1519648166.43	17017336690.17	1701733669.02	122925.27	2615431.35	130771.57
30 May 2018 17:05	WARWICK	Mick Maestro	3	1.27	164.72	475473661.57	18536984856.60	1853698485.66	36967.81	2738356.63	136917.83
30 May 2018 17:40	WARWICK	Whatduhavtoget	1	0.00	164.72	-1806183559.23	19012458518.17	1901245851.82	-138766.22	2775324.44	138766.22
30 May 2018 18:35	RIPON	Rockin Roy	2	1.24	164.94	392303069.06	17206274958.94	1720627495.89	31638.70	2636558.22	131827.91
30 May 2018 19:05	RIPON	Weellan	1	1.29	165.22	484840824.67	17598578028.01	1759857802.80	38688.86	2668196.92	133409.85
30 May 2018 19:50	WARWICK	Royalraise	2	1.35	165.55	601273676.85	18083418852.68	1808341885.27	47370.50	2706885.77	135344.29
31 May 2018 13:50	WOLVERHAMPTON	Musical Art	3	1.09	165.64	159754121.13	18684692529.53	1868469252.95	12394.15	2754256.28	137712.81
31 May 2018 14:00	HAMILTON	Big Ace	1	1.38	166.00	680284524.09	18844446650.66	1884444665.07	52566.36	2766650.43	138332.52
31 May 2018 14:30	HAMILTON	Jabbarockie	2	1.67	166.64	1242749139.27	19524731174.75	1952473117.47	94443.76	2819216.79	140960.84
31 May 2018 16:40	LINGFIELD	Red Island	2	1.30	166.92	591873188.95	20767480314.02	2076748031.40	43704.91	2913660.55	[illegible]
31 May 2018 18:10	CHELMSFORD (A.W)	Buckingham	1	1.30	[illegible]	791304047.28	21359353502.97	2135935350.30	57668.63	2957365.46	147868.27
31 May 2018 19:10	CHELMSFORD (A.W)	Vale Of Kent	3	1.63	167.89	1325720445.38	22150717550.25	2215071755.03	94973.57	3015034.08	150751.70
01 Jun 2018 14:25	CATTERICK	St Malo	1	1.27	168.13	602170634.59	23476437995.64	2347643799.56	41985.10	3110007.66	155500.38
01 Jun 2018 15:00	CATTERICK	Eeh Bah Gum	1	1.09	168.23	205872103.79	24078608630.22	2407860863.02	14183.97	3151992.76	157599.64
01 Jun 2018 15:10	EPSOM	Cracksman	1	1.13	168.36	299913337.07	24284480734.01	2428448073.40	20580.15	3166176.73	158308.84
01 Jun 2018 16:10	CATTERICK	Brockholes	1	1.45	168.79	1050982846.54	24584394071.08	2458439407.11	71702.03	3186756.88	159337.84
01 Jun 2018 16:30	EPSOM	Wild Illusion	2	1.69	169.44	1680398956.95	25635376917.62	2563537691.76	112416.83	3258458.91	162922.95
01 Jun 2018 18:10	GOODWOOD	Pretty Jewel	1	1.57	169.98	1479149263.61	27315775874.57	2731577587.46	96069.96	3370875.74	168543.79
01 Jun 2018 18:20	BATH	High Horse	2	1.14	170.11	382972504.34	28794925138.17	2879492513.82	24268.62	3466945.70	173347.28
01 Jun 2018 18:40	GOODWOOD	Main Edition	1	1.24	170.34	665256066.25	29177897642.51	2917789764.25	41894.57	3491214.32	174560.72
01 Jun 2018 19:25	BATH	Breanski	2	1.46	170.77	1304145817.07	29843153708.76	2984315370.88	81261.50	3533108.89	176655.44
01 Jun 2018 19:35	DONCASTER	Spanish City	1	1.33	171.09	976467840.13	31147299525.83	3114729952.58	59637.11	3614370.39	180718.52
01 Jun 2018 20:50	GOODWOOD	Ganayem	1	1.29	171.36	885009790.93	32123767365.97	3212376736.60	53273.11	3674007.51	183700.38
02 Jun 2018 15:30	WORCESTER	Black Kalanisi	1	1.34	171.68	1066183502.17	33008777156.90	3300877715.69	63363.77	3727280.61	186364.03
02 Jun 2018 16:05	WORCESTER	Earth Moor	2	1.34	172.01	1100621229.29	34074960659.07	3407496065.91	64440.95	3790644.38	189532.22
02 Jun 2018 17:25	DONCASTER	Sam Gold	1	1.23	172.22	768586464.26	35175581888.36	3517558188.84	44333.48	3855085.34	192754.27
02 Jun 2018 18:10	LINGFIELD (A.W)	Midnight Blue	1	1.22	172.43	751233118.57	35944168352.62	3594416835.26	42893.61	3899418.82	194970.94
02 Jun 2018 19:00	CHEPSTOW	Shaybani	1	1.31	172.73	1080679573.33	36695401471.19	3669540147.12	61105.84	3942312.43	197115.62
02 Jun 2018 19:10	LINGFIELD	Miss Elsa	2	1.12	172.85	430647323.91	37776081044.51	3777608104.45	24020.51	4003418.27	200170.91
02 Jun 2018 19:40	LINGFIELD	Bellevarde	1	1.60	173.42	2177783517.00	38206728368.42	3820672836.84	120823.16	4027438.78	201371.94
02 Jun 2018 20:00	CHEPSTOW	Flying Sparkle	1	1.27	173.67	1035862729.86	40384511885.42	4038451188.54	56001.54	4148261.94	207413.10
04 Jun 2018 14:10	LEICESTER	Two Blondes	3	1.38	174.03	1495275523.61	41420374615.28	4142037461.53	79881.01	4204263.48	210213.17
04 Jun 2018 14:40	LEICESTER	Acrux	1	1.32	174.34	1304635764.22	42915650138.89	4291565013.89	68546.31	4284144.49	214207.22
04 Jun 2018 16:10	LEICESTER	Global Conquero	1	1.12	174.45	504111259.30	44220285903.12	4422028590.31	26116.14	4352690.80	217634.54
04 Jun 2018 16:50	NEWTON ABBOT	Free Stone Hill	2	2.12	175.52	4758675858.08	44724397162.41	4472439716.24	245213.19	4378806.94	218940.35
04 Jun 2018 18:00	AYR	Dream Today	2	1.09	175.60	423080274.33	49483073020.49	4948307302.05	20808.09	4624020.13	231201.01
04 Jun 2018 18:15	WINDSOR	Queen Of Bermu	1	1.18	175.77	853395221.34	49906153294.82	4990615329.48	41803.45	4644828.22	232241.41
04 Jun 2018 18:45	WINDSOR	Buffer Zone	1	1.21	175.98	1012652992.90	50759548516.16	5075954851.62	49209.63	4686631.68	234331.58
04 Jun 2018 19:45	WINDSOR	What A Welcome	1	1.38	176.34	1868976474.48	51772201509.05	5177220150.91	89980.98	4735841.31	236792.07
05 Jun 2018 14:15	FONTWELL	Westerbee	3	1.56	176.87	2853710668.72	53641177983.53	5364117798.35	135123.02	4825822.29	241291.11
05 Jun 2018 21:05	SOUTHWELL	Lady Marwah	3	1.54	177.39	2898187787.86	56494888652.26	5649488865.23	133945.52	4960945.32	248047.27
06 Jun 2018 14:30	HAMILTON	Jonboy	2	1.46	177.82	2595477440.43	59393076440.12	5939307644.01	117182.49	5094890.84	254744.54
06 Jun 2018 15:40	UTTOXETER	Stradivarius Davi	3	1.07	176.82	412223883.31	61988553880.55	6198855388.05	18242.26	5212073.33	260603.67
06 Jun 2018 16:10	UTTOXETER	Salix	1	1.54	177.34	3201159899.29	62400777763.86	6240077776.39	141218.52	5230315.59	261515.78
06 Jun 2018 16:20	WOLVERHAMPTON	Mischief Manage	3	1.57	177.88	3552344924.46	65601937663.14	6560193766.31	152088.72	5371534.11	268576.71
06 Jun 2018 16:50	WOLVERHAMPTON	Pride's Gold	1	1.21	178.08	1379627937.62	69154282587.60	6915428258.76	58008.54	5524622.83	276231.14
06 Jun 2018 17:00	HAMILTON	Only Spoofing	1	1.09	178.16	603064934.99	70533910525.22	7053391052.52	25121.84	5582631.37	279131.57
06 Jun 2018 17:20	WOLVERHAMPTON	Azpeitia	2	1.43	178.57	2905945447.55	71136975460.21	7113697546.02	120566.69	5607753.21	[illegible]
06 Jun 2018 18:00	KEMPTON (A.W)	Beyond Reason	1	1.17	[illegible]	1193793172.66	74042920907.76	7404292090.78	48690.72	5728319.90	286416.00
06 Jun 2018 19:30	KEMPTON (A.W)	Insurgence	1	1.57	179.27	4074176367.45	75238714080.42	7523871408.04	164644.80	5777010.62	288850.53
07 Jun 2018 14:00	HAYDOCK	Airmax	3	1.38	179.63	2863195345.17	79312890447.88	7931289044.79	112891.45	5941655.43	297082.77
07 Jun 2018 14:20	YARMOUTH	Blonde Warrior	1	1.08	179.71	624538252.03	82176085793.05	8217608579.30	24218.19	6054546.88	302727.34
07 Jun 2018 14:30	HAYDOCK	Angel's Hideawa	1	1.15	179.86	1179908892.64	82800624045.07	8280062404.51	45590.74	6078765.07	303938.25
07 Jun 2018 15:00	HAYDOCK	Soldiers Call	1	1.11	179.96	877596569.20	83980532937.72	8398053293.77	33683.96	6124355.81	306217.79
07 Jun 2018 16:20	YARMOUTH	Hombre Casado	1	1.52	180.46	4191991597.64	84858129506.92	8485812950.69	160109.03	6158039.76	307901.99
07 Jun 2018 16:30	HAYDOCK	Mystic Flight	1	1.09	180.55	761378535.44	89050121104.56	8905012110.46	28431.67	6318148.80	315907.44
07 Jun 2018 16:40	RIPON	Savaanah	1	1.11	180.65	938530171.24	89811499640.00	8981149964.00	34906.19	6346580.47	317329.02
07 Jun 2018 16:50	YARMOUTH	Marilyn	1	1.15	180.80	1293187924.81	90750029811.24	9075002981.12	47861.15	6381486.66	319074.33
07 Jun 2018 19:35	SANDOWN	Corgi	1	1.64	181.41	5596227638.35	92043217736.05	9204321773.60	205739.13	6429347.81	321467.39
07 Jun 2018 19:45	CARLISLE	French Resistanc	1	1.60	181.98	5565448386.34	97639445374.40	9763944537.44	199052.61	6635086.94	331754.35
07 Jun 2018 20:20	CARLISLE	Fujaira Prince	1	1.07	182.04	686312543.51	103204893760.74	10320489376.07	23919.49	6834139.55	341706.98
07 Jun 2018 20:50	CARLISLE	Florencio	2	2.00	182.99	9869664598.90	103891206304.25	10389120630.43	342902.95	6858059.03	342902.95
08 Jun 2018 15:10	BRIGHTON	Mamillius	3	1.76	183.71	8213534879.21	113760870903.15	11376087090.32	273636.56	7200961.99	360048.10
08 Jun 2018 16:10	BRIGHTON	Braemar	2	1.23	183.93	2665140766.34	121974405782.36	12197440578.24	85957.88	7474598.54	373729.93
08 Jun 2018 18:30	GOODWOOD	Oeil De Tigre	1	1.26	184.18	3078596799.75	124639546548.71	12463954654.87	98287.23	7560556.42	378027.82
08 Jun 2018 19:25	HAYDOCK	Presidential	1	1.53	184.68	6430608517.59	127718143348.46	12771814334.85	202959.36	7658843.66	382942.18
08 Jun 2018 21:10	HAYDOCK	Lamloom	3	1.34	185.01	4333004685.27	134148751866.06	13414875186.61	133050.65	7861803.02	393090.15
09 Jun 2018 14:05	BEVERLEY	Alhahaal	1	1.48	185.46	6314768098.74	138481756551.33	13848175655.13	191890.89	7995453.67	399772.68
09 Jun 2018 14:50	HAYDOCK	God Given	1	1.54	185.97	7428061714.55	144796524650.07	14479652465.01	221058.30	8187344.55	409367.23

THE HORSE RACING PLACE BET INVESTMENT STRATEGY

09 Jun 2018 14:55	CATTERICK	Sellingallthetime	2	1.49	186.43	7086054495.27	152224586364.62	15222458636.46	206005.87	8408402.86	420420.14
09 Jun 2018 15:10	MUSSELBURGH	Ballistic	3	1.57	185.43	8626671202.56	159310640859.89	15931064085.99	245510.65	8614408.73	430720.44
09 Jun 2018 16:05	CATTERICK	Italian Riviera	1	1.27	185.69	4307592054.40	167937312062.45	16793731206.25	119608.91	8859919.38	442995.97
09 Jun 2018 16:15	NEWMARKET (JULY)	Aim Of Artemis	1	1.22	185.90	3599918496.04	172244904116.86	17224490411.69	98774.81	8979528.29	448976.41
09 Jun 2018 16:40	CATTERICK	Weellan	2	1.68	186.55	11359575540.79	175844822612.90	17584482261.29	308662.31	9078303.10	453915.15
09 Jun 2018 18:35	STRATFORD	Imperial Presenc	1	2.11	187.60	19740703785.31	187204398153.69	18720439815.37	520976.58	9386965.40	469348.27
10 Jun 2018 13:45	NOTTINGHAM	Napanook	3	1.41	186.60	8060511720.52	206945101939.00	20694510193.90	203112.81	9907941.98	495397.10
11 Jun 2018 14:30	BRIGHTON	More Than Likely	1	1.40	186.99	8170213319.06	215005613659.52	21500561365.95	202221.10	10111054.80	505552.74
11 Jun 2018 17:15	WORCESTER	Mr Mafia	1	1.81	187.75	17173379886.00	223175826978.58	22317582697.86	417687.67	10313275.89	515663.79
12 Jun 2018 15:00	SALISBURY	Pilot Wings	3	1.33	188.07	7534947635.20	240349206864.59	24034920686.46	177060.90	10730963.56	536548.18
12 Jun 2018 16:15	THIRSK	Mutafani	1	1.08	188.15	1883919574.20	247884154499.79	24788415449.98	43632.10	10908024.46	545401.22
12 Jun 2018 17:15	THIRSK	Mutabaahy	1	1.34	188.47	8067508792.59	249768074073.99	24976807407.40	186178.16	10951656.56	547582.83
12 Jun 2018 19:20	LINGFIELD	Howman	1	1.18	188.64	4408988467.02	257835582866.58	25783558286.66	100240.51	11137834.72	556891.74
12 Jun 2018 20:40	SOUTHWELL	Je Suis Charlie	1	1.33	188.95	8221367311.31	262244571333.60	26224457133.36	185428.24	11238075.24	561903.76
13 Jun 2018 14:20	CHELMSFORD (A.W)	I'll Have Another	1	1.22	189.16	5652738117.68	270465938644.91	27046593864.49	125658.54	11423503.48	571175.17
13 Jun 2018 14:50	CHELMSFORD (A.W)	Red Island	1	1.31	189.45	8131695030.66	276118676762.58	27611867676.26	179012.01	11549162.01	577458.10
13 Jun 2018 16:10	HAYDOCK	New Society	3	1.69	190.11	18632611871.05	284250371793.24	28425037179.32	404622.00	11728174.03	586408.70
13 Jun 2018 17:30	YARMOUTH	De Vegas Kid	1	1.70	190.77	20141718413.68	302882983664.29	30288298366.43	424647.86	12132796.03	606639.80
13 Jun 2018 19:30	HAMILTON	Mr Wagyu	1	1.13	190.90	3989355070.66	323024702077.96	32302470207.80	81623.39	12557443.89	627872.19
14 Jun 2018 14:10	NOTTINGHAM	Zain City	1	1.11	191.00	3417296897.20	327014057148.63	32701405714.86	69514.87	12639067.28	631953.36
14 Jun 2018 14:20	NEWBURY	Watheeqa	2	1.37	191.35	11614662094.71	330431354045.83	33043135404.58	235108.77	12708582.15	635429.11
14 Jun 2018 14:40	NOTTINGHAM	Sharamm	1	1.04	191.39	1299774861.33	342046016140.54	34204601614.05	25887.38	12943690.92	647184.55
14 Jun 2018 21:15	UTTOXETER	Keep The River	1	1.23	191.61	7502105533.39	343345791001.88	34334579100.19	149150.15	12969578.30	648478.91
15 Jun 2018 13:50	YORK	Chapelli	1	1.37	191.96	12332303563.21	350847896535.27	35084789653.53	242696.48	13118728.45	655936.42
15 Jun 2018 14:55	YORK	Mr Buttons	2	1.47	192.41	16215995934.40	363180200098.48	36318020009.85	313993.49	13361424.92	668071.25
15 Jun 2018 16:30	NEWTON ABBOT	Passing Call	2	1.11	192.51	3964690248.54	379396196032.88	37939619603.29	75214.80	13675418.41	683770.92
15 Jun 2018 16:50	SANDOWN	Beringer	1	1.45	192.94	16388677888.53	383360886281.42	38336088628.14	309389.25	13750633.21	687531.66
15 Jun 2018 17:15	YORK	Zeelander	2	1.15	193.08	5696431289.42	399749564169.95	39974956417.00	105450.17	14060022.46	703001.12
15 Jun 2018 19:00	CHEPSTOW	Dashing Poet	1	1.30	193.36	11555210870.59	405445995459.37	40544599545.94	212482.09	14165472.63	708273.63
15 Jun 2018 19:20	AINTREE	Cause Toujours	1	1.27	193.62	10696080942.36	417001206329.97	41700120633.00	194102.39	14377954.72	718897.74
15 Jun 2018 20:35	CHEPSTOW	Queen Of Conna	3	1.39	193.99	15846184493.44	427697287272.33	42769728727.23	284155.11	14572057.11	728602.86
15 Jun 2018 20:45	GOODWOOD	Saroog	1	1.17	194.15	7163227069.02	443543471765.77	44354347176.58	126277.80	14856212.22	742810.61
16 Jun 2018 15:20	HEXHAM	The Unit	1	1.10	194.24	4281713638.93	450706698834.79	45070669883.48	74912.45	14982490.02	749124.50
16 Jun 2018 15:30	BATH	Swift And Sure	2	1.32	194.55	13831647739.20	454988412473.72	45498841247.37	240918.44	15057402.47	752870.12
16 Jun 2018 16:30	HEXHAM	Second Time Aro	2	1.68	195.19	30285775889.75	468820060212.92	46882006021.29	520142.91	15298320.91	764916.05
16 Jun 2018 18:10	LEICESTER	Chaleur	1	1.22	195.41	10431311974.55	499105836102.67	49910583610.27	174003.10	15818463.82	790923.19
16 Jun 2018 20:25	FONTWELL	Mrsrobin	1	1.42	195.80	20330532208.28	509537148077.22	50953714807.72	335841.81	15992466.93	799623.35
16 Jun 2018 20:40	LEICESTER	Panko	1	1.43	196.21	21645094739.66	529867680285.50	52986768028.55	351058.64	16328308.73	816415.44
17 Jun 2018 14:10	DONCASTER	Storm Ahead	3	1.69	196.87	36151662402.90	551512775025.16	55151277502.52	575438.17	16679367.37	833968.37
17 Jun 2018 14:25	SALISBURY	Wicked Sea	1	1.39	197.24	21772967406.71	587664437428.06	58766443742.81	336468.71	17254805.54	862740.28
17 Jun 2018 14:40	DONCASTER	Aussie View	1	1.64	197.84	37053794213.95	609437404834.77	60943740483.48	562920.78	17591274.25	879563.71
17 Jun 2018 15:25	SALISBURY	Gumriyah	1	1.21	198.04	12897499421.02	646491199048.72	64649119904.87	190619.05	18154195.03	907709.75
18 Jun 2018 14:00	AYR	Society Queen	1	1.03	198.07	1879257790.64	659388698469.75	65938869846.97	27517.22	18344814.07	917240.70
18 Jun 2018 21:00	WINDSOR	Rock Eagle	1	1.06	198.13	3769227350.68	661267956260.39	66126795626.04	55116.99	18372331.30	918616.56
19 Jun 2018 14:20	STRATFORD	Grageelagh Girl	1	1.10	198.22	6317853244.31	665037183611.07	66503718361.11	92137.24	18427448.29	921372.41
19 Jun 2018 15:20	THIRSK	Beauty Filly	2	1.25	198.46	15944682125.32	671355036855.38	67135503685.54	231494.82	18519585.53	925979.28
19 Jun 2018 17:10	THIRSK	Kawasir	2	1.08	198.54	5223477864.25	687299718980.69	68729971898.07	75004.32	18751080.35	937554.02
19 Jun 2018 19:40	BRIGHTON	Seinesational	1	1.31	198.83	20394808147.08	692523196844.94	69252319684.49	291804.31	18826084.67	941304.23
19 Jun 2018 20:40	BRIGHTON	Ask The Guru	3	1.70	199.49	47409047331.97	712918004992.03	71291800499.20	669126.11	19117888.98	955894.45
20 Jun 2018 13:40	HAMILTON	I Believe In You	1	1.56	200.02	40449399183.64	760327052324.00	76032705232.40	554036.42	19787015.10	989350.75
20 Jun 2018 14:10	HAMILTON	Sense Of Belongi	3	1.21	199.02	15975490207.58	800776451507.63	80077645150.76	213581.04	20341051.52	1017052.58
20 Jun 2018 16:20	ASCOT	Cracksman	2	1.25	199.27	19397858615.74	816751941715.21	81675194171.52	256932.91	20554632.56	1027731.63
20 Jun 2018 16:35	HAMILTON	Vive La Differenc	1	1.30	199.55	23830269309.43	836149800330.95	83614980033.09	312173.48	20811565.47	1040578.27
20 Jun 2018 17:45	HAMILTON	Competition	3	1.18	199.72	14705659190.85	859980069640.38	85998006964.04	190113.65	21123738.95	1056186.95
20 Jun 2018 21:20	RIPON	Hula Girl	3	1.18	199.89	14957125963.01	874685728831.23	87468572883.12	191824.67	21313852.60	1065692.63
21 Jun 2018 15:40	ASCOT	Wild Illusion	2	1.56	200.42	47328999875.05	889642854794.24	88964285479.42	602158.96	21505677.28	1075283.86
21 Jun 2018 15:55	RIPON	Daira Prince	1	1.47	200.86	41835793310.98	936971854669.30	93697185466.93	519534.15	22107836.24	1105391.81
21 Jun 2018 16:05	CHELMSFORD (A.W)	Shailene	1	1.15	201.01	13948008983.72	978807647980.28	97880764798.03	169705.28	22627370.39	1131368.52
21 Jun 2018 19:45	FFOS LAS	The Bottom Bar	3	1.31	200.01	29236654097.59	992755656964.00	99275565696.40	353354.67	22797075.67	1139853.78
22 Jun 2018 14:20	REDCAR	Showroom	1	1.11	200.11	10679819650.59	###############	##############	127327.37	23150430.34	1157521.52
22 Jun 2018 17:10	MARKET RASEN	Fortunes Hiding	3	1.13	200.23	12753500814.30	###############	##############	151305.43	23277757.71	1163887.89
22 Jun 2018 17:35	ASCOT	Dash Of Spice	1	2.00	201.18	99315434995.02	###############	##############	1171453.16	23429063.13	1171453.16
22 Jun 2018 18:10	WETHERBY	Poetic Steps	2	1.78	201.92	84825313029.24	###############	##############	959420.14	24600516.29	1230025.81
22 Jun 2018 18:55	NEWMARKET (JULY)	Alnasherat	3	1.20	202.12	23361761211.46	###############	##############	255599.36	25559936.43	1277996.82
23 Jun 2018 13:45	AYR	Chuck Willis	1	1.43	202.53	51182114550.14	###############	##############	555034.02	25815535.79	1290776.79
23 Jun 2018 16:00	NEWMARKET (JULY)	Red Starlight	1	1.63	203.13	78050998780.44	###############	##############	830672.95	26370569.81	1318528.49
23 Jun 2018 17:05	PERTH	Tanarpino	2	1.12	203.24	15756638296.66	###############	##############	163207.46	27201242.76	1360062.14
23 Jun 2018 17:15	REDCAR	Worship	2	1.22	203.45	29216483950.94	###############	##############	301008.95	27364450.21	1368222.51
23 Jun 2018 19:15	HAYDOCK	More Than This	1	1.39	203.82	52875328643.41	###############	##############	539476.45	27665459.17	1383272.96
23 Jun 2018 20:00	LINGFIELD	Critical Data	1	1.11	203.92	15466101417.08	###############	##############	155127.15	28204935.62	1410246.78
23 Jun 2018 20:45	HAYDOCK	Strategist	2	1.19	204.10	26993338305.54	###############	##############	269420.60	28360062.77	1418003.14
23 Jun 2018 21:00	LINGFIELD	Dragon Moon	1	1.22	204.31	31819605124.36	###############	##############	314924.32	28629483.36	1431474.17
24 Jun 2018 14:20	HEXHAM	Caius Marcius	2	1.09	204.39	13289168811.05	###############	##############	130249.83	28944407.68	1447220.38
24 Jun 2018 15:10	WORCESTER	Destiny's Gold	1	1.14	204.52	20848786317.94	###############	##############	203522.60	29074657.51	1453732.88
24 Jun 2018 16:50	HEXHAM	Gonn Away	2	1.36	204.86	54324193309.62	###############	##############	527007.24	29278180.12	1463909.01
25 Jun 2018 14:15	SOUTHWELL	Lotus Pond	1	1.15	205.01	23409200300.34	###############	##############	223538.91	29805187.36	1490259.37
25 Jun 2018 15:30	CHEPSTOW	Madame Jo Jo	2	1.27	205.26	42737006528.31	###############	##############	405387.80	30028726.26	1501436.31
25 Jun 2018 15:45	SOUTHWELL	Artful Artist	1	1.11	205.37	17857974748.27	###############	##############	167387.63	30434114.07	1521705.70
25 Jun 2018 16:45	SOUTHWELL	Simply Lucky	3	1.46	205.81	75459196989.28	###############	##############	703834.54	30601501.70	1530075.08
25 Jun 2018 20:20	WOLVERHAMPTON (	Moqarrab	1	1.16	205.96	27393657007.90	###############	##############	250442.69	31305336.24	1565266.81
25 Jun 2018 20:40	WINDSOR	Worth Waiting	1	1.28	206.22	48667571040.24	###############	##############	441780.90	31555778.93	1577788.95
25 Jun 2018 21:10	WINDSOR	Kaanoon	1	1.39	206.60	69590107455.94	###############	##############	623952.42	31997559.83	1599877.99
26 Jun 2018 14:00	BEVERLEY	Victory Comman	1	1.03	206.62	5551416995.17	###############	##############	48932.27	32621512.25	1631075.61
26 Jun 2018 19:00	NEWTON ABBOT	Double Treasure	1	1.25	206.86	46393654446.70	###############	##############	408380.56	32670444.52	1633522.23
27 Jun 2018 14:50	WORCESTER	Monbeg Legend	2	1.40	207.24	75992805983.70	###############	##############	661576.50	33078825.07	1653941.25
27 Jun 2018 17:20	WORCESTER	Black Kalanisi	1	1.50	207.71	98600665763.85	###############	##############	843510.04	33740401.57	1687020.08
27 Jun 2018 17:50	BATH	Winged Spur	1	1.35	208.04	72298938171.34	###############	##############	605218.45	34583911.61	1729195.58
27 Jun 2018 18:10	KEMPTON (A.W)	Spirit Kingdom	1	1.34	208.37	72568509926.52	###############	##############	598215.21	35189130.07	1759456.50
27 Jun 2018 18:40	KEMPTON (A.W)	Sporting Chance	2	1.20	208.56	44066160468.91	###############	##############	357873.45	35787345.28	1789367.26

THE HORSE RACING PLACE BET INVESTMENT STRATEGY

28 Jun 2018 14:30	NEWCASTLE (A.W)	Amadeus Grey	2	1.18	208.73	40413075766.04	###############	##############	325306.97	36145218.73	1807260.94
28 Jun 2018 15:15	NEWMARKET (JULY)	Glenglade	2	1.21	208.93	47954829255.25	###############	##############	382940.52	36470525.70	1823526.28
28 Jun 2018 15:25	NOTTINGHAM	Mainsail Atlantic	2	1.25	209.17	58228009641.53	###############	##############	460668.33	36853466.22	1842673.31
28 Jun 2018 17:45	NOTTINGHAM	Ravenhoe	2	1.53	209.67	126375160725.50	###############	##############	988824.57	37314134.55	1865706.73
28 Jun 2018 19:35	HAMILTON	Desert Fire	1	1.21	209.87	52594361347.71	###############	##############	402181.07	38302959.11	1915147.96
28 Jun 2018 21:10	HAMILTON	Mujassam	1	2.20	211.01	306534964894.84	###############	##############	2322308.41	38705140.18	1935257.01
29 Jun 2018 14:40	YARMOUTH	Autumn Splendo	1	1.04	211.04	11382665029.76	###############	##############	82054.90	41027448.59	2051372.43
29 Jun 2018 15:00	DONCASTER	Blonde Warrior	1	1.05	211.09	14282398946.09	###############	##############	102773.76	41109503.49	2055475.17
29 Jun 2018 15:20	CARTMEL	Souriyan	1	1.07	211.16	20090336477.52	###############	##############	144242.97	41212277.25	2060613.86
29 Jun 2018 19:20	NEWMARKET (JULY)	Midnight Blue	2	1.53	211.66	153124096057.17	###############	##############	1095947.79	41356520.22	2067826.01
29 Jun 2018 20:15	CHESTER	Gossip Column	1	1.47	212.11	142626283618.89	###############	##############	997633.00	42452468.01	2122623.40
29 Jun 2018 21:00	NEWMARKET (JULY)	Escalator	1	1.32	212.41	101443095954.03	###############	##############	695201.62	43450101.00	2172505.05
29 Jun 2018 21:10	NEWCASTLE (A.W)	Oriental Lilly	1	1.63	213.01	205787464452.34	###############	##############	1390577.03	44145302.62	2207265.13
30 Jun 2018 13:35	YORK	Dunkerron	1	1.57	213.55	197332049514.12	###############	##############	1297772.57	45535879.65	2276793.98
30 Jun 2018 13:50	WINDSOR	Indian Sounds	3	1.30	213.84	109482936839.64	###############	##############	702504.78	46833652.22	2341682.61
30 Jun 2018 13:55	CHESTER	Beauty Filly	3	1.25	212.84	93836000449.64	###############	##############	594201.96	47536157.01	2376807.85
30 Jun 2018 14:20	NEWMARKET (JULY)	Moyassar	2	1.25	213.08	96064605460.32	###############	##############	601629.49	48130358.97	2406517.95
30 Jun 2018 14:30	CHESTER	Tanasoq	1	1.32	213.38	125883058995.20	###############	##############	779711.82	48731988.46	2436599.42
30 Jun 2018 15:00	WINDSOR	Come On Leicest	2	1.08	213.46	32427475997.16	###############	##############	198046.80	49511700.27	2475585.01
30 Jun 2018 15:40	CHESTER	Gabrial The Wire	1	1.13	213.58	53095127823.95	###############	##############	323113.36	49709747.07	2485487.35
30 Jun 2018 15:50	NEWCASTLE (A.W)	Ventura Ocean	2	1.13	213.70	53750852652.50	###############	##############	325213.59	50032860.43	2501643.02
30 Jun 2018 19:00	DONCASTER	Tashaaboh	1	1.11	213.81	46043187116.25	###############	##############	276969.41	50358074.02	2517903.70
30 Jun 2018 19:15	LINGFIELD	Implicit	2	1.15	213.95	63442279665.84	###############	##############	379762.83	50635043.43	2531752.17
01 Jul 2018 13:30	UTTOXETER	Celestial Path	1	1.40	214.33	171590219069.53	###############	##############	1020296.13	51014806.25	2550740.31
01 Jul 2018 14:10	CARTMEL	Secret Escape	1	1.12	214.44	53433194218.25	###############	##############	312210.61	52035102.38	2601755.12
01 Jul 2018 14:25	WINDSOR	Goodnight Girl	1	1.11	214.55	49538804912.98	###############	##############	287910.22	52347312.99	2617365.65
01 Jul 2018 14:35	UTTOXETER	Fair Mountain	1	1.09	214.63	40955306256.26	###############	##############	236858.50	52635223.21	2631761.16
01 Jul 2018 15:10	UTTOXETER	Symphony Of An	1	1.63	215.23	289138318873.27	###############	##############	1665470.57	52872081.72	2643604.09
01 Jul 2018 15:35	WINDSOR	Argentello	1	1.10	215.33	48641785279.02	###############	##############	272687.76	54537552.29	2726877.61
02 Jul 2018 14:30	PONTEFRACT	Blown By Wind	1	1.09	215.41	44193494015.26	###############	##############	246646.08	54810240.05	2740512.00
02 Jul 2018 14:45	WOLVERHAMPTON (	Water Diviner	1	1.24	215.64	118856929037.56	###############	##############	660682.63	55056886.13	2752844.31
02 Jul 2018 15:00	PONTEFRACT	Bambino Lola	1	1.28	215.90	141828011522.89	###############	##############	780045.96	55717568.77	2705070.44
02 Jul 2018 15:30	PONTEFRACT	Construct	1	1.10	216.05	83200363788.23	###############	##############	451980.92	56497614.73	2824880.74
02 Jul 2018 18:30	WINDSOR	Ginger Nut	1	1.51	216.54	269232217200.51	###############	##############	1452214.69	56949595.65	2847479.78
02 Jul 2018 18:45	HAMILTON	I Believe In You	1	1.19	216.71	105161840085.37	###############	##############	554817.20	58401810.34	2920090.52
02 Jul 2018 20:45	HAMILTON	Isabella	2	1.70	217.38	394431620574.92	###############	##############	2063481.96	58956627.54	2947831.38
03 Jul 2018 14:00	BRIGHTON	Monarch Maid	3	1.47	216.38	282444031387.54	###############	##############	1433972.57	61020109.50	3051005.47
03 Jul 2018 14:15	HAMILTON	Zebzardee	3	1.12	215.38	75333231673.79	###############	##############	374724.49	62454082.07	3122704.10
03 Jul 2018 14:45	HAMILTON	Where's Jeff	1	1.22	215.59	139685389277.26	###############	##############	691116.87	62828806.56	3141440.33
03 Jul 2018 15:00	BRIGHTON	Fitzsimmons	1	1.06	215.65	38892221976.31	###############	##############	190559.77	63519923.44	3175996.17
03 Jul 2018 16:00	BRIGHTON	Matchmaking	1	1.12	215.76	78227815283.16	###############	##############	382262.90	63710483.21	3185524.16
03 Jul 2018 16:45	HAMILTON	The Great Wall	1	1.68	216.41	448344470138.52	###############	##############	2179153.37	64092746.11	3204637.31
03 Jul 2018 17:00	BRIGHTON	Jack Taylor	1	1.14	216.54	98269195893.13	###############	##############	463903.30	66271899.47	3313594.97
03 Jul 2018 18:30	STRATFORD	Hatcher	1	1.22	216.75	156476848311.94	###############	##############	734093.83	66735802.77	3336790.14
03 Jul 2018 20:45	CHEPSTOW	Happy Ending	3	1.64	217.36	464719169284.82	###############	##############	2159036.69	67469896.60	3373494.83
04 Jul 2018 15:10	WORCESTER	Skin Deep	1	1.13	217.48	100135363001.65	###############	##############	452588.07	69628933.29	3481446.66
04 Jul 2018 16:20	THIRSK	History Writer	3	1.18	217.65	140361278863.45	###############	##############	630733.69	70081521.36	3504076.07
04 Jul 2018 18:50	KEMPTON (A.W)	Pilaster	1	1.26	217.90	206210993057.36	###############	##############	919259.32	70712255.05	3535612.75
04 Jul 2018 19:10	BATH	Queen Of Desire	1	1.04	217.94	32508369936.29	###############	##############	143263.03	71631514.37	3581575.72
04 Jul 2018 19:40	BATH	Vale Of Kent	1	0.00	217.94	###############	###############	##############	-3588738.87	71774777.40	3588738.87
04 Jul 2018 20:10	BATH	Altra Vita	1	1.17	218.10	125510452075.35	###############	##############	579581.33	68186038.53	3409301.93
04 Jul 2018 20:40	BATH	Groveman	1	1.17	218.26	127537445876.36	###############	##############	584507.77	68765619.85	3438280.99
05 Jul 2018 15:50	YARMOUTH	Austin Powers	1	1.71	218.93	541258792325.64	###############	##############	2461929.53	69350127.62	3467506.38
05 Jul 2018 17:40	NEWBURY	Iconic Knight	1	1.20	219.10	162751182498.03	###############	##############	718120.57	71812057.15	3590602.86
05 Jul 2018 18:30	EPSOM	Arden Warrior	2	1.11	219.23	91213900231.02	###############	##############	398915.98	72530177.72	3626508.89
05 Jul 2018 18:45	NEWBURY	Almurr	1	1.31	219.52	259743604558.32	###############	##############	1130400.95	72929093.70	3646454.69
05 Jul 2018 20:40	EPSOM	Rock Icon	3	1.44	218.52	379525624624.28	###############	##############	1629308.88	74059494.65	3702974.73
06 Jul 2018 14:50	NEWTON ABBOT	Sword Of Fate	1	1.44	218.94	395389795733.57	###############	##############	1665153.68	75688803.54	3784440.18
06 Jul 2018 15:10	DONCASTER	Hajjam	2	1.57	219.48	533619865548.38	###############	##############	2204587.78	77353957.21	3867697.86
06 Jul 2018 15:55	NEWTON ABBOT	Tamarillo Grove	2	1.64	220.09	631596217563.87	###############	##############	2545873.44	79558544.99	3977927.25
06 Jul 2018 16:20	DONCASTER	Bombyx	1	1.08	220.17	83749658448.97	###############	##############	328417.67	82104418.43	4105220.92
06 Jul 2018 17:05	NEWTON ABBOT	Full Bore	1	1.21	220.37	221513659114.60	###############	##############	865544.78	[illegible]	[illegible]
06 Jul 2018 17:15	SANDOWN	Michele Strogoff	[illegible]	[illegible]	[illegible]	[illegible]	###############	##############	2124108.71	83298380.89	4164919.04
06 Jul 2018 19:20	HAYDOCK	Auxerre	1	1.12	220.96	135359602009.65	###############	##############	512534.94	85422489.60	4271124.48
06 Jul 2018 19:45	BEVERLEY	Delph Crescent	1	1.23	221.18	262396844489.07	###############	##############	[illegible]	[illegible]	4296751.23
07 Jul 2018 13:35	CHELMSFORD (A.W)	[illegible]	3	1.54	220.18	629523114748.79	###############	##############	2346928.49	86923277.32	4346163.87
07 Jul 2018 14:00	BEVERLEY	Prince Elzaam	2	1.48	220.64	588282356031.47	###############	##############	2142484.94	89270205.81	4463510.29
07 Jul 2018 14:35	BEVERLEY	Thriving	1	1.16	220.79	205036010488.84	###############	##############	731301.53	[illegible]	[illegible]
07 Jul 2018 15:00	LEICESTER	Railport Dolly	3	1.51	221.27	668486278141.35	###############	##############	2349671.80	92143992.27	4607199.61
07 Jul 2018 16:05	HAYDOCK	Epaulement	2	1.73	221.97	995708818571.82	###############	##############	3449018.74	94493664.08	4724683.20
07 Jul 2018 16:25	CHELMSFORD (A.W)	Global Wonder	2	1.58	222.52	845974672028.86	###############	##############	2840337.80	97942682.81	4897134.14
07 Jul 2018 16:50	BEVERLEY	Winged Spur	2	1.44	222.93	677135630416.15	###############	##############	2217226.45	100783020.62	5039151.03
07 Jul 2018 21:00	CARLISLE	Arcadian Cat	3	1.09	221.93	144294524952.45	###############	##############	463501.11	103000247.07	5150012.35
08 Jul 2018 14:45	MARKET RASEN	Yensir	1	1.30	222.22	485094143802.65	###############	##############	1551956.22	103463748.18	5173187.41
08 Jul 2018 16:05	AYR	Ventura Knight	1	1.34	222.54	565441903821.17	###############	##############	1785266.97	105015704.40	5250785.22
09 Jul 2018 17:40	WINDSOR	Letmestopyouthe	3	1.38	222.90	[illegible]	###############	##############	2029218.46	106800971.38	5340048.57
09 Jul 2018 19:30	RIPON	Ad Libitum	1	1.60	223.47	###############	###############	##############	3264905.70	108830189.84	5441509.49
09 Jul 2018 20:10	WINDSOR	King's Slipper	1	1.16	223.62	300823419785.78	###############	##############	896760.76	112095095.53	5604754.78
09 Jul 2018 21:00	RIPON	Restive Spirit	1	1.10	223.72	190872459854.08	###############	##############	[illegible]	[illegible]	[illegible]
10 Jul 2018 16:00	PONTEFRACT	[illegible]	[illegible]	1.00	223.79	154148598578.15	###############	##############	454227.26	113556815.58	5677840.78
10 Jul 2018 16:45	WOLVERHAMPTON (	Move Swiftly	1	1.13	223.92	252395207881.94	###############	##############	741071.78	114011042.84	5700552.14
10 Jul 2018 17:15	WOLVERHAMPTON (	Tobruk	1	1.28	224.18	550334160275.38	###############	##############	1606529.60	114752114.62	5737605.73
10 Jul 2018 18:00	UTTOXETER	Eric The Third	1	1.27	224.44	544795440048.04	###############	##############	1570841.70	116358644.22	5817932.21
10 Jul 2018 19:10	BRIGHTON	Genetics	1	1.25	224.68	517379113967.84	###############	##############	1474118.57	117929485.92	5896474.30
10 Jul 2018 19:30	UTTOXETER	Movie Set	3	0.00	223.68	###############	###############	##############	-5970180.22	119403604.49	5970180.22
10 Jul 2018 20:00	UTTOXETER	Equus Flight	3	1.13	223.80	249261228045.31	###############	##############	737317.26	113433424.27	5671671.21
10 Jul 2018 20:40	BRIGHTON	Bombshell Bay	1	1.39	224.17	757018812635.00	###############	##############	2226329.46	114170741.53	5708537.08
11 Jul 2018 14:30	LINGFIELD	Full Suit	1	1.61	224.75	###############	###############	##############	3550110.67	116397070.99	5819853.55
11 Jul 2018 14:40	CATTERICK	Artarmon	1	1.48	225.21	###############	###############	##############	2878732.36	119947181.65	5997359.08

THE HORSE RACING PLACE BET INVESTMENT STRATEGY

11 Jul 2018 14:50	YARMOUTH	Pink Iceburg	1	1.13	225.33	289478178246.95	###############	###############	798368.44	122825914.01	6141295.70
11 Jul 2018 15:10	CATTERICK	Prairie Spy	3	1.21	224.33	473393685285.72	###############	###############	1298054.97	123624282.45	6181214.12
11 Jul 2018 15:40	CATTERICK	Montague	1	1.31	224.63	712760693739.15	###############	###############	1936296.23	124922337.42	6246116.87
11 Jul 2018 16:00	LINGFIELD	North Korea	1	2.32	225.89	###############	###############	###############	8372669.82	126858633.65	6342931.68
11 Jul 2018 16:20	YARMOUTH	Excelleration	2	1.13	226.01	346288101266.55	###############	###############	879003.47	135231303.47	6761565.17
11 Jul 2018 16:55	YARMOUTH	Arendelle	3	1.13	225.01	350564759317.19	###############	###############	884717.00	136110306.94	6805515.35
11 Jul 2018 17:55	KEMPTON (A.W)	Divine Messenge	2	1.89	225.86	###############	###############	###############	6096278.57	136995023.93	6849751.20
11 Jul 2018 18:10	BATH	Final Rock	1	1.09	225.94	266469605714.40	###############	###############	643910.86	143091302.50	7154565.13
11 Jul 2018 18:40	BATH	Archimedes	3	1.58	226.50	###############	###############	###############	4168321.19	143735213.36	7186760.67
11 Jul 2018 21:10	BATH	Jaganory	3	1.45	226.92	###############	###############	###############	3327829.53	147903534.55	7395176.73
12 Jul 2018 14:25	NEWMARKET (JULY)	Advertise	1	1.19	227.11	624208999948.48	###############	###############	1436697.96	151231364.08	7561568.20
12 Jul 2018 17:00	CARLISLE	Dizzy G	1	1.31	227.40	###############	###############	###############	2366354.96	152668062.03	7633403.10
12 Jul 2018 18:00	EPSOM	Dubai Legacy	1	1.07	227.47	241017640973.29	###############	###############	542620.46	155034417.00	7751720.85
12 Jul 2018 18:25	NEWBURY	Fox Coach	2	1.27	227.72	935821574816.53	###############	###############	2100290.01	155577037.46	7778851.87
12 Jul 2018 20:45	EPSOM	Careyanne	3	1.37	228.07	###############	###############	###############	2917030.56	157677327.46	7883866.37
13 Jul 2018 14:15	ASCOT	Dirty Rascal	2	1.41	228.46	###############	###############	###############	3292184.34	160594358.02	8029717.90
13 Jul 2018 15:35	NEWMARKET (JULY)	Alpha Centauri	1	1.22	228.67	841102818495.68	###############	###############	1802751.97	163886542.36	8194327.12
13 Jul 2018 17:10	ASCOT	Simply Breathles	3	2.00	229.62	###############	###############	###############	8284464.72	165689294.32	8284464.72
13 Jul 2018 17:30	YORK	Byron's Choice	1	2.00	230.57	###############	###############	###############	8698687.95	173973759.04	8698687.95
13 Jul 2018 18:10	CHEPSTOW	Nazzaa	3	1.22	229.57	###############	###############	###############	2009396.92	182672446.99	9133622.35
13 Jul 2018 18:40	CHEPSTOW	Street Parade	1	1.25	229.81	###############	###############	###############	2308523.05	184681843.91	9234092.20
14 Jul 2018 13:50	ASCOT	Mendoza	3	1.43	230.22	###############	###############	###############	4020292.89	186990366.96	9349518.35
14 Jul 2018 15:45	CHESTER	King Lud	2	1.55	230.74	###############	###############	###############	5252793.15	191010659.85	9550532.99
14 Jul 2018 16:10	ASCOT	Prevent	2	2.41	232.08	###############	###############	###############	13836573.44	196263452.99	9813172.65
14 Jul 2018 16:15	YORK	Northwest Fronti	1	1.39	232.46	###############	###############	###############	4096950.52	210100026.43	10505001.32
14 Jul 2018 16:50	YORK	He'Zanarab	3	1.95	233.36	###############	###############	###############	10174356.40	214196976.95	10709848.85
14 Jul 2018 17:35	NEWTON ABBOT	Sea Of Mystery	3	1.66	233.99	###############	###############	###############	7404254.00	224371333.35	11218566.67
14 Jul 2018 17:45	SALISBURY	Duke Of Hazzard	2	1.66	234.62	###############	###############	###############	7648594.38	231775587.35	11588779.37
14 Jul 2018 18:00	HAMILTON	Woodside Wond	1	1.29	234.89	###############	###############	###############	3471650.64	239424181.73	11971209.09
14 Jul 2018 18:30	HAMILTON	Alsvinder	1	1.45	235.32	###############	###############	###############	5465156.23	242895832.37	12144791.62
14 Jul 2018 18:45	SALISBURY	Bedouin's Story	1	1.19	235.51	###############	###############	###############	2359429.39	248360988.60	12418049.43
14 Jul 2018 20:45	SALISBURY	Savaanah	1	0.00	235.51	###############	###############	###############	-12536020.90	250720417.99	12536020.90
15 Jul 2018 14:40	STRATFORD	One For Billy	1	1.30	235.79	###############	###############	###############	3572765.96	238184397.09	11909219.85
15 Jul 2018 15:15	STRATFORD	Hatcher	1	1.08	235.86	630025662113.39	###############	###############	967028.65	241757163.05	12087858.15
15 Jul 2018 15:55	SOUTHWELL	Robin Des Mana	1	1.12	235.98	952220785718.17	###############	###############	1456345.15	242724191.70	12136209.58
15 Jul 2018 16:10	PERTH	Grageelagh Girl	3	1.09	236.06	722307077006.52	###############	###############	1098812.42	244180536.85	12209026.84
15 Jul 2018 16:50	STRATFORD	Two Hoots	2	1.63	236.66	###############	###############	###############	7726299.50	245279349.26	12263967.46
16 Jul 2018 14:15	RIPON	Three Card Trick	2	1.14	236.79	###############	###############	###############	1771039.54	253005648.77	12650282.44
16 Jul 2018 16:55	RIPON	Snow Wind	1	1.21	236.99	###############	###############	###############	2675155.23	254776688.31	12738834.42
16 Jul 2018 18:20	WINDSOR	Magical Wish	1	1.16	237.15	###############	###############	###############	2059614.75	257451843.53	12872592.18
16 Jul 2018 19:50	WINDSOR	Mouchee	1	1.36	237.48	###############	###############	###############	4671206.25	259511458.28	12975572.91
16 Jul 2018 20:10	WOLVERHAMPTON	Real Estate	2	1.16	237.63	###############	###############	###############	2113461.32	264182664.53	13209133.23
17 Jul 2018 15:40	BATH	Show Stealer	1	1.15	237.78	###############	###############	###############	1997220.94	266296125.85	13314806.29
17 Jul 2018 17:50	WORCESTER	Dark Invader	1	1.95	238.68	###############	###############	###############	12743933.97	268293346.79	13414667.34
17 Jul 2018 18:10	THIRSK	Addis Ababa	2	1.19	238.86	###############	###############	###############	2669854.17	281037280.76	14051864.04
17 Jul 2018 19:40	THIRSK	Sharp Style	1	1.13	238.98	###############	###############	###############	1844096.38	283707134.93	14185356.75
17 Jul 2018 20:50	WORCESTER	G For Ginger	1	1.51	239.46	###############	###############	###############	7281556.40	285551231.31	14277561.57
18 Jul 2018 13:40	LINGFIELD (A.W)	Indian Warrior	2	1.56	239.99	###############	###############	###############	8199318.06	292832787.71	14641639.39
18 Jul 2018 15:40	LINGFIELD	Its'afreebee	1	1.20	240.19	###############	###############	###############	3010321.06	301032105.76	15051605.29
18 Jul 2018 16:30	CATTERICK	Alsvinder	1	1.55	240.71	###############	###############	###############	8361166.74	304042426.82	15202121.34
18 Jul 2018 16:40	LINGFIELD	Francophilia	3	1.37	239.71	###############	###############	###############	5779466.48	312403593.56	15620179.68
18 Jul 2018 16:50	UTTOXETER	Longhouse Sale	1	1.11	239.81	###############	###############	###############	1750006.83	318183060.04	15909153.00
18 Jul 2018 17:10	LINGFIELD	Trouble And Strif	1	0.00	239.81	###############	###############	###############	-15996653.34	319933066.87	15996653.34
18 Jul 2018 18:10	YARMOUTH	Persian Moon	1	1.33	240.13	###############	###############	###############	5014950.82	303936413.53	15196820.68
18 Jul 2018 18:55	WOLVERHAMPTON	Indian Tygress	2	1.15	240.27	###############	###############	###############	2317135.23	308951364.35	15447568.22
18 Jul 2018 19:30	WOLVERHAMPTON	Spring Romance	2	1.25	240.51	###############	###############	###############	3890856.24	311268499.58	15563424.98
18 Jul 2018 20:00	WOLVERHAMPTON	Penny Poet	2	1.91	241.37	###############	###############	###############	14339750.69	315159355.83	15757967.79
19 Jul 2018 14:00	HAMILTON	Space Traveller	1	1.06	241.43	842638246934.83	###############	###############	988497.32	329499106.52	16474955.33
19 Jul 2018 14:20	LEICESTER	Desert Fire	1	1.02	241.45	282480428314.12	###############	###############	330487.60	330487603.84	16524380.19
19 Jul 2018 15:00	HAMILTON	Gullane One	1	1.50	241.92	###############	###############	###############	8270452.29	330818091.44	16540904.57
19 Jul 2018 15:10	CHEPSTOW	Rockin Roy	1	1.12	242.03	###############	###############	###############	2034531.26	339088543.73	16954427.19
19 Jul 2018 15:40	CHEPSTOW	Gold Hunter	3	1.38	241.03	###############	###############	###############	6481338.42	341123074.99	17056153.75
19 Jul 2018 15:50	LEICESTER	Island Cloud	1	1.68	241.68	###############	###############	###############	11818550.06	347604413.41	17380220.67
19 Jul 2018 16:30	HAMILTON	Warmhearted	1	1.17	241.84	###############	###############	###############	3055095.19	359422963.47	17971148.17
19 Jul 2018 17:15	CHEPSTOW	Show Of Force	1	1.95	242.74	###############	###############	###############	17217707.79	362478058.66	18123902.93
19 Jul 2018 17:55	EPSOM	Duke Of North	1	1.57	243.28	###############	###############	###############	10821329.34	379695766.45	18984788.32
19 Jul 2018 20:45	EPSOM	Hyanna	1	1.23	243.50	###############	###############	###############	4490946.60	390517095.79	19525854.79
19 Jul 2018 21:05	DONCASTER	Sister Celine	3	1.72	242.50	###############	###############	###############	14220289.53	395008042.39	19750402.12
20 Jul 2018 13:50	NOTTINGHAM	Loch Ness Monst	1	1.07	242.56	###############	###############	###############	1432299.16	409228331.92	20461416.60
20 Jul 2018 15:25	NOTTINGHAM	Thimbleweed	1	1.13	242.69	###############	###############	###############	2669294.10	410660631.08	20533031.55
20 Jul 2018 16:30	NOTTINGHAM	Aquarium	1	0.00	242.69	###############	###############	###############	-20666496.26	413329925.18	20666496.26
20 Jul 2018 16:40	NEWBURY	Majboor	1	1.40	243.07	###############	###############	###############	7853268.58	392663428.92	19633171.45
20 Jul 2018 16:50	HAYDOCK	Surya	1	1.57	243.61	###############	###############	###############	11414725.88	400516697.50	20025834.87
20 Jul 2018 18:20	HAMILTON	Showout	1	1.08	243.69	###############	###############	###############	1647725.69	411931423.38	20596571.17
20 Jul 2018 19:00	PONTEFRACT	Mobham	3	1.21	242.69	###############	###############	###############	4342581.07	413579149.07	20678957.45
20 Jul 2018 20:25	HAMILTON	Atticus Boy	1	1.27	242.95	###############	###############	###############	5641943.36	417921730.14	20896086.51
21 Jul 2018 13:35	MARKET RASEN	Stole The Show	1	1.07	243.01	###############	###############	###############	1482472.86	423563673.49	21178183.67
21 Jul 2018 14:30	CARTMEL	Wells De Lune	1	1.85	243.82	###############	###############	###############	18064461.22	425046146.35	21252307.32
21 Jul 2018 14:55	RIPON	Eljayeff	1	1.11	243.92	###############	###############	###############	2437108.34	443110607.57	22155530.38
21 Jul 2018 15:00	NEWBURY	Projection	2	1.72	244.61	###############	###############	###############	16039717.77	445547715.91	22277385.80
21 Jul 2018 18:30	HAYDOCK	Line of Duty	2	1.18	244.78	###############	###############	###############	4154286.90	461587433.69	23079371.68
22 Jul 2018 13:50	NEWTON ABBOT	Cotton Club	2	1.11	244.88	###############	###############	###############	2561579.46	465741720.59	23287086.03
22 Jul 2018 14:10	STRATFORD	Leapaway	1	1.11	244.99	###############	###############	###############	2575668.15	468303300.05	23415165.00
22 Jul 2018 15:00	NEWTON ABBOT	Tidal Watch	1	1.18	245.16	###############	###############	###############	4237910.71	470878968.20	23543948.41
22 Jul 2018 15:45	REDCAR	Whinmoor	1	1.38	245.52	###############	###############	###############	9027220.70	475116878.92	23755843.95
22 Jul 2018 15:55	STRATFORD	Vosne Romanee	1	1.41	245.91	###############	###############	###############	9924954.04	484144099.62	24207204.98
23 Jul 2018 13:30	AYR	Axe Axelrod	2	1.04	245.95	###############	###############	###############	988138.11	494069053.66	24703452.68
23 Jul 2018 18:10	WINDSOR	Happy Odyssey	2	1.53	246.45	###############	###############	###############	13119015.58	495057191.76	24752859.59
23 Jul 2018 18:30	BEVERLEY	Queen Jo Jo	1	1.16	246.61	###############	###############	###############	4065409.66	508176207.35	25408810.37

THE HORSE RACING PLACE BET INVESTMENT STRATEGY

23 Jul 2018 20:10	WINDSOR	Klassique	1	1.12	246.72	###############	###############	##############	3073449.70	512241617.01	25612080.85
24 Jul 2018 14:10	NEWCASTLE (A.W)	Louis Treize	1	1.21	246.92	###############	###############	##############	5410808.20	515315066.71	25765753.34
24 Jul 2018 14:30	FFOS LAS	Fox Tal	1	1.23	247.14	###############	###############	##############	5988347.56	520725874.91	26036293.75
24 Jul 2018 14:50	MUSSELBURGH	Kilbarchan	1	1.40	247.52	###############	###############	##############	10534284.45	526714222.47	26335711.12
24 Jul 2018 15:05	FFOS LAS	Anchises	2	1.11	247.63	###############	###############	##############	2954866.79	537248506.92	26862425.35
24 Jul 2018 15:45	NEWCASTLE (A.W)	Mister Ambassad	1	1.29	247.91	###############	###############	##############	7832948.92	540203373.71	27010168.69
24 Jul 2018 17:10	FFOS LAS	Jashma	1	1.37	248.26	###############	###############	##############	10138671.97	548036322.63	27401816.13
24 Jul 2018 18:40	CHELMSFORD (A.W)	Moyassar	1	1.09	248.35	###############	###############	##############	2511787.48	558174994.59	27908749.73
24 Jul 2018 20:10	CHELMSFORD (A.W)	Piece Of History	1	1.33	248.66	###############	###############	##############	9251331.90	560686782.07	28034339.10
25 Jul 2018 15:10	CATTERICK	Jfoul	1	1.35	248.99	###############	###############	##############	9973916.99	569938113.97	28496905.70
25 Jul 2018 15:40	CATTERICK	Sultan Baybars	3	1.27	247.99	###############	###############	##############	7828812.42	579912030.97	28995601.55
25 Jul 2018 15:50	LINGFIELD	Sea Fox	1	1.28	248.26	###############	###############	##############	8228371.81	587740843.39	29387042.17
25 Jul 2018 17:30	LEICESTER	Champagne Bob	1	1.62	248.85	###############	###############	##############	18475045.67	595969215.19	29798460.76
26 Jul 2018 15:15	WORCESTER	G For Ginger	3	1.70	247.85	###############	###############	##############	21505549.13	614444260.86	30722213.04
26 Jul 2018 15:45	WORCESTER	Drovers Lane	1	1.08	247.92	###############	###############	##############	2543799.24	635949810.00	31797490.50
26 Jul 2018 16:20	WORCESTER	The Twisler	1	1.09	248.01	###############	###############	##############	2873221.24	638493609.24	31924680.46
26 Jul 2018 18:10	NEWBURY	Legends Of War	1	1.06	248.07	###############	###############	##############	1924100.49	641366830.48	32068341.52
26 Jul 2018 18:40	NEWBURY	Star Terms	1	1.35	248.40	###############	###############	##############	11257591.29	643290930.97	32164546.55
26 Jul 2018 19:30	DONCASTER	Rapier	1	1.45	248.82	###############	###############	##############	14727341.75	654548522.26	32727426.11
26 Jul 2018 20:20	NEWBURY	Goodnight Girl	1	1.35	249.15	###############	###############	##############	11712327.62	669275864.01	33463793.20
27 Jul 2018 14:00	THIRSK	Dream Of Honou	2	1.28	249.47	###############	###############	##############	9533834.68	680988191.63	34049409.58
27 Jul 2018 15:10	THIRSK	Super Major	1	1.54	249.93	###############	###############	##############	18644094.71	690522026.31	34526101.32
27 Jul 2018 16:30	UTTOXETER	King's Reste	1	1.43	250.34	###############	###############	##############	15247071.60	709166121.02	35458306.05
27 Jul 2018 17:05	UTTOXETER	Full Bore	2	1.45	250.77	###############	###############	##############	16299296.83	724413192.63	36220659.63
27 Jul 2018 19:00	YORK	Persian Moon	1	1.43	251.17	###############	###############	##############	15925318.52	740712489.46	37035624.47
27 Jul 2018 19:20	CHEPSTOW	Glamorous Drear	1	1.38	251.53	###############	###############	##############	14376118.35	756637807.98	37831890.40
27 Jul 2018 19:40	NEWMARKET (JULY)	Fairlight	1	0.00	251.53	###############	###############	##############	-38550696.32	771013926.34	38550696.32
27 Jul 2018 20:20	CHEPSTOW	Timoshenko	1	1.16	251.68	###############	###############	##############	5859705.84	732463230.02	36623161.50
28 Jul 2018 13:40	NEWCASTLE (A.W)	Something Brewi	3	1.79	252.43	###############	###############	##############	29163755.97	738322935.86	36916146.79
28 Jul 2018 13:50	ASCOT	Royal Interventic	2	1.57	252.97	###############	###############	##############	21873370.72	767486691.83	38374334.58
28 Jul 2018 14:15	NEWMARKET (JULY)	Dubai Dominion	1	1.56	[illegible]	###############	###############	##############	22102081.75	789360062.54	39468003.13
28 Jul 2018 15:10	CHESTER	Powerallied	1	1.20	253.69	###############	###############	##############	8114621.44	811462144.39	40573107.21
28 Jul 2018 15:55	NEWCASTLE (A.W)	Lucky Lucky Man	1	1.30	254.00	###############	###############	##############	15571958.55	819576765.74	40978838.29
28 Jul 2018 16:15	ASCOT	Nate The Great	3	1.50	253.06	###############	###############	##############	20878718.11	835148724.29	41757436.21
28 Jul 2018 17:35	YORK	Deputise	3	1.83	252.06	###############	###############	##############	35525138.86	856027442.39	42801372.12
28 Jul 2018 19:00	LINGFIELD	Concierge	1	1.03	252.08	###############	###############	##############	1337328.87	891552581.25	44577629.06
28 Jul 2018 19:15	SALISBURY	Prevent	2	1.52	252.58	###############	###############	##############	23215137.66	892889910.12	44644495.51
28 Jul 2018 19:45	SALISBURY	Midnight Meetin	1	1.07	252.64	###############	###############	##############	3206367.67	916105047.79	45805252.39
28 Jul 2018 20:30	LINGFIELD	Flying Sakhee	2	1.29	252.92	###############	###############	##############	13330015.52	919311415.45	45965570.77
29 Jul 2018 13:50	WOLVERHAMPTON (	Penny Poet	3	1.70	253.58	###############	###############	##############	32642450.08	932641430.98	46632071.55
29 Jul 2018 14:00	PONTEFRACT	Flawless Jewel	1	1.04	253.62	###############	###############	##############	1930567.76	965283881.06	48264194.05
29 Jul 2018 14:30	PONTEFRACT	Multellie	1	1.22	253.83	###############	###############	##############	10639358.94	967214448.82	48360722.44
29 Jul 2018 14:50	WOLVERHAMPTON (	Documenting	1	1.39	254.20	###############	###############	##############	19068149.25	977853807.76	48892690.39
29 Jul 2018 15:10	UTTOXETER	Golden Birthday	2	1.71	254.87	###############	###############	##############	35390729.47	996921957.01	49846097.85
29 Jul 2018 16:35	PONTEFRACT	Rock Force	3	1.20	255.06	###############	###############	##############	10323126.86	############	51615634.32
30 Jul 2018 13:20	LINGFIELD (A.W)	Shorter Skirt	2	1.39	255.43	###############	###############	##############	20331398.36	############	52131790.67
30 Jul 2018 14:40	NEWTON ABBOT	Mister Fizz	1	1.36	255.78	###############	###############	##############	19133409.81	############	53148360.59
30 Jul 2018 15:50	LINGFIELD (A.W)	Twister	2	1.23	256.00	###############	###############	##############	12444157.15	############	54105031.08
30 Jul 2018 16:20	LINGFIELD (A.W)	Ben Vrackie	1	1.11	256.10	###############	###############	##############	6019996.28	############	54727238.93
30 Jul 2018 17:10	WOLVERHAMPTON (	Implicit	1	1.32	256.41	###############	###############	##############	17609036.40	############	55028238.75
30 Jul 2018 17:45	WOLVERHAMPTON (	Rockin Roy	1	1.08	256.48	###############	###############	##############	4472695.25	############	55908690.57
30 Jul 2018 20:20	WINDSOR	Makambe	3	1.34	256.81	###############	###############	##############	19084990.61	############	56132325.33
31 Jul 2018 15:15	BEVERLEY	Northernpowerh	3	1.30	257.10	###############	###############	##############	17125972.46	############	57086574.86
31 Jul 2018 15:25	YARMOUTH	Final Rock	1	1.28	257.36	###############	###############	##############	16224004.58	############	57942873.48
31 Jul 2018 16:20	BEVERLEY	Three Saints Bay	1	1.53	257.86	###############	###############	##############	31139659.07	############	58754073.71
31 Jul 2018 18:05	WORCESTER	Brave Eagle	1	1.26	258.11	###############	###############	##############	15680874.73	############	60311056.67
31 Jul 2018 20:50	WORCESTER	Carntop	1	1.14	258.24	###############	###############	##############	8553314.06	############	61095100.40
01 Aug 2018 13:30	PERTH	Portrush Ted	1	1.06	258.30	###############	###############	##############	3691365.97	############	61522766.11
01 Aug 2018 15:00	GOODWOOD	Soldier's Call	3	1.39	258.67	###############	###############	##############	24065860.42	############	61707334.40
01 Aug 2018 18:05	LEICESTER	Golden Force	2	1.33	258.99	###############	###############	##############	20760507.05	############	62910627.42
02 Aug 2018 13:30	STRATFORD	Hatcher	1	1.06	259.04	###############	###############	##############	3836919.17	############	63948652.78
02 Aug 2018 13:50	GOODWOOD	Communique	1	2.00	259.99	###############	###############	##############	64140498.74	############	[illegible]
02 Aug 2018 15:20	NOTTINGHAM	Urban Arnest	1	1.11	260.10	###############	###############	##############	7408227.60	############	67347523.67
02 Aug 2018 16:30	NOTTINGHAM	Jack Regan	1	1.33	260.41	###############	###############	##############	22346918.57	############	67717935.05
02 Aug 2018 17:20	GOODWOOD	Cowboy Soldier	3	2.00	261.36	###############	###############	##############	[illegible]	############	68835280.98
02 Aug 2018 18:40	FFOS LAS	[illegible]	2	1.07	261.42	###############	###############	##############	5059393.15	############	72277045.03
02 Aug 2018 18:55	EPSOM	Mendoza	3	1.16	260.42	###############	###############	##############	11604802.35	############	72530014.69
02 Aug 2018 19:15	FFOS LAS	Sweet Pursuit	1	1.56	260.96	###############	###############	##############	40941742.69	############	73110254.00
03 Aug 2018 13:50	GOODWOOD	Mirage Dancer	1	1.47	261.41	###############	###############	##############	35323950.71	############	75157341.94
03 Aug 2018 15:35	GOODWOOD	Battaash	1	1.23	261.62	###############	###############	##############	17692414.08	############	76923539.47
03 Aug 2018 16:30	THIRSK	Fairy Falcon	1	1.28	261.89	###############	###############	##############	21786284.85	############	77808160.18
03 Aug 2018 17:35	THIRSK	Letmestopyouthe	2	1.13	262.01	###############	###############	##############	10256671.67	############	78897474.42
03 Aug 2018 18:00	WOLVERHAMPTON (	Island Of Life	3	1.16	262.16	###############	###############	##############	12705649.28	############	79410308.00
04 Aug 2018 14:15	THIRSK	Major Partnershi	1	1.10	262.26	###############	###############	##############	8004559.05	############	80045590.47
04 Aug 2018 15:00	GOODWOOD	Dee Ex Bee	2	1.47	262.71	###############	###############	##############	37809534.66	############	80445818.42
04 Aug 2018 17:45	DONCASTER	Penny Pot Lane	3	1.68	263.36	###############	###############	##############	55988680.70	############	82336295.15
04 Aug 2018 18:20	HAMILTON	Angel's Glory	2	1.09	263.44	###############	###############	##############	7662215.63	############	85135729.19
04 Aug 2018 18:35	LINGFIELD	Critical Data	3	1.16	263.59	###############	###############	##############	13683014.40	############	85518839.97
05 Aug 2018 13:50	CHESTER	Quiet Endeavour	1	1.39	263.96	###############	###############	##############	33619166.37	############	86202990.69
05 Aug 2018 14:25	CHESTER	The Trader	1	1.11	264.06	###############	###############	##############	9667234.39	############	87883949.01
05 Aug 2018 17:20	MARKET RASEN	Longhouse Sale	1	1.10	264.16	###############	###############	##############	8836731.07	############	88367310.73
06 Aug 2018 14:00	RIPON	Evie Speed	1	1.38	264.52	###############	###############	##############	33747475.97	############	88809147.28
06 Aug 2018 14:20	NEWTON ABBOT	Angel Of Harlem	3	1.74	265.22	###############	###############	##############	66967425.60	############	90496521.08
06 Aug 2018 15:30	RIPON	Sheepscar Lad	2	1.81	265.98	###############	###############	##############	76014362.81	############	93844892.36
06 Aug 2018 17:00	RIPON	Volcanic Sky	2	1.24	266.21	###############	###############	##############	23434946.52	############	97645610.50
06 Aug 2018 18:00	WINDSOR	Lively Lydia	1	1.22	266.42	###############	###############	##############	21739818.72	############	98817357.83
06 Aug 2018 19:00	WINDSOR	George Villiers	2	1.92	267.29	###############	###############	##############	91912000.86	############	99904348.76
07 Aug 2018 14:50	NEWBURY	Hot Team	1	1.09	267.38	###############	###############	##############	9404995.39	############	###########
07 Aug 2018 17:40	AYR	Fognini	2	1.26	267.62	###############	###############	##############	27292251.63	############	###########

THE HORSE RACING PLACE BET INVESTMENT STRATEGY

07 Aug 2018 18:45	AYR	Dark Defender	3	2.03	266.62	###############	###############	###############	109524855.49	############	###########
07 Aug 2018 19:15	AYR	Play Mate	3	1.22	265.62	###############	###############	###############	24598431.87	############	###########
07 Aug 2018 19:25	NOTTINGHAM	Archie Perkins	2	1.62	266.21	###############	###############	###############	70085404.83	############	###########
07 Aug 2018 20:30	NOTTINGHAM	Daffy Jane	1	1.80	266.97	###############	###############	###############	93236196.61	############	###########
07 Aug 2018 20:50	AYR	Ana Lichious	1	1.69	267.63	###############	###############	###############	83632868.36	############	###########
08 Aug 2018 14:10	BRIGHTON	Big Baby Bull	1	1.41	268.02	###############	###############	###############	51409366.60	############	###########
08 Aug 2018 14:20	PONTEFRACT	Final Rock	2	1.15	268.16	###############	###############	###############	19193875.10	############	###########
08 Aug 2018 14:30	CHEPSTOW	Sir Victor	1	1.06	268.22	###############	###############	###############	7735131.67	############	###########
08 Aug 2018 18:40	KEMPTON (A.W)	Nawar	3	1.46	268.66	###############	###############	###############	59480584.13	############	###########
08 Aug 2018 19:40	KEMPTON (A.W)	Elasia	1	1.24	268.89	###############	###############	###############	31747115.25	############	###########
08 Aug 2018 20:20	YARMOUTH	Letmestopyouth	1	1.24	269.12	###############	###############	###############	32128080.64	############	###########
09 Aug 2018 14:00	BRIGHTON	Wiley Post	1	1.72	269.80	###############	###############	###############	97540852.81	############	###########
09 Aug 2018 14:20	YARMOUTH	Marhaba Milliar	1	1.16	269.95	###############	###############	###############	22456071.89	############	###########
09 Aug 2018 14:40	HAYDOCK	Moyassar	2	1.09	270.04	###############	###############	###############	12732592.76	############	###########
09 Aug 2018 16:50	YARMOUTH	La Isla Bonita	1	1.43	270.44	###############	###############	###############	61107249.50	############	###########
09 Aug 2018 17:45	NEWCASTLE (A.W)	Kilbarchan	2	1.41	270.83	###############	###############	###############	59517750.46	############	###########
09 Aug 2018 19:10	SANDOWN	Jack Regan	2	1.76	271.56	###############	###############	###############	112587260.74	############	###########
10 Aug 2018 13:50	WOLVERHAMPTON (	Magical Wish	2	1.10	271.65	###############	###############	###############	15377049.56	############	###########
10 Aug 2018 18:15	HAYDOCK	Beatboxer	1	1.07	271.71	###############	###############	###############	10817754.36	############	###########
10 Aug 2018 19:00	CHELMSFORD (A.W)	Broken Spear	2	1.38	272.07	###############	###############	###############	58930489.60	############	###########
10 Aug 2018 19:20	HAYDOCK	Dark Thunder	2	1.65	272.69	###############	###############	###############	102717394.18	############	###########
11 Aug 2018 13:30	CHELMSFORD (A.W)	Toffee Galore	2	1.22	272.90	###############	###############	###############	35895778.60	############	###########
11 Aug 2018 15:10	NEWMARKET (JULY)	Danceteria	1	1.46	273.34	###############	###############	###############	75880412.70	############	###########
11 Aug 2018 17:10	LINGFIELD	Matchmaking	3	1.32	272.34	###############	###############	###############	54000460.65	############	###########
11 Aug 2018 17:45	LINGFIELD	Spirit Of Appin	1	1.08	272.41	###############	###############	###############	13716117.01	############	###########
11 Aug 2018 18:15	LINGFIELD	Global Warning	2	1.27	272.67	###############	###############	###############	46477062.48	############	###########
11 Aug 2018 19:45	LINGFIELD	Vegas Boy	1	1.66	273.30	###############	###############	###############	115144340.22	############	###########
11 Aug 2018 20:15	LINGFIELD	Aaliya	1	1.23	273.51	###############	###############	###############	41450217.87	############	###########
12 Aug 2018 16:35	WINDSOR	Madame Bounty	2	1.66	274.14	###############	###############	###############	120311960.64	############	###########
13 Aug 2018 14:20	RIPON	Mrs Hoo	1	1.47	274.59	###############	###############	###############	88504030.32	############	###########
13 Aug 2018 14:40	AYR	Acadian Angel	3	1.73	275.28	###############	###############	###############	140694103.77	############	###########
13 Aug 2018 16:15	AYR	Bossipop	2	1.71	275.95	###############	###############	###############	141834111.48	############	###########
13 Aug 2018 18:30	WINDSOR	Greeley	1	2.16	277.06	###############	###############	###############	239955349.33	############	###########
13 Aug 2018 19:10	WOLVERHAMPTON (	Penarth Pier	1	1.39	277.43	###############	###############	###############	85353772.62	############	###########
13 Aug 2018 20:00	WINDSOR	Dubai Silk	3	1.13	277.55	###############	###############	###############	29006057.06	############	###########
14 Aug 2018 14:00	CHELMSFORD (A.W)	Seductive	2	1.53	278.06	###############	###############	###############	119024123.92	############	###########
14 Aug 2018 14:30	CHELMSFORD (A.W)	Ummalnar	1	1.03	278.09	###############	###############	###############	6915750.75	############	###########
14 Aug 2018 16:30	CHELMSFORD (A.W)	Cowboy Soldier	2	1.24	278.32	###############	###############	###############	55408994.99	############	###########
14 Aug 2018 17:05	NOTTINGHAM	Orobas	1	1.74	279.02	###############	###############	###############	172894534.03	############	###########
14 Aug 2018 18:20	THIRSK	Stronsay	1	1.76	279.74	###############	###############	###############	184137351.56	############	###########
15 Aug 2018 14:20	NEWTON ABBOT	Cracker Factory	1	1.08	279.82	###############	###############	###############	20119428.52	############	###########
15 Aug 2018 14:50	NEWTON ABBOT	Mister Fizz	1	1.43	280.23	###############	###############	###############	108574496.00	############	###########
15 Aug 2018 15:00	BEVERLEY	Jacbequick	1	1.57	280.77	###############	###############	###############	147018705.04	############	###########
15 Aug 2018 15:50	NEWTON ABBOT	Chantecler	2	1.32	281.08	###############	###############	###############	84889116.15	############	###########
15 Aug 2018 17:00	BEVERLEY	Our Little Pony	1	1.61	281.66	###############	###############	###############	164408995.69	############	###########
15 Aug 2018 17:20	WORCESTER	Master Sunrise	3	1.50	282.13	###############	###############	###############	138871696.77	############	###########
15 Aug 2018 18:30	KEMPTON (A.W)	Quiet Endeavour	1	1.38	282.49	###############	###############	###############	108181051.79	############	###########
15 Aug 2018 19:20	WORCESTER	Desirable Court	3	1.19	281.49	###############	###############	###############	55118245.89	############	###########
15 Aug 2018 19:30	KEMPTON (A.W)	Angel's Glory	1	1.16	281.65	###############	###############	###############	46856310.92	############	###########
16 Aug 2018 13:20	WOLVERHAMPTON (	Axe Axelrod	1	1.72	282.33	###############	###############	###############	212540226.35	############	###########
16 Aug 2018 14:00	BEVERLEY	Glass Slippers	1	1.31	282.62	###############	###############	###############	94804748.74	############	###########
16 Aug 2018 17:10	SALISBURY	Winds Of Fire	1	1.22	282.83	###############	###############	###############	68323641.67	############	###########
16 Aug 2018 18:10	CHEPSTOW	Dancing On A Dr	2	1.34	283.16	###############	###############	###############	106752584.48	############	###########
17 Aug 2018 15:40	NOTTINGHAM	Tiffin Top	2	1.31	283.45	###############	###############	###############	98987903.85	############	###########
17 Aug 2018 16:20	WOLVERHAMPTON (	Al Mureib	2	1.30	283.73	###############	###############	###############	97279564.22	############	###########
17 Aug 2018 16:35	NEWBURY	Alhakmah	2	1.21	283.93	###############	###############	###############	69117130.38	############	###########
17 Aug 2018 17:25	NEWMARKET (JULY)	Indian Viceroy	1	1.09	284.02	###############	###############	###############	29932654.39	############	###########
17 Aug 2018 18:20	CHELMSFORD (A.W)	One To Go	2	1.22	284.23	###############	###############	###############	73497969.93	############	###########
17 Aug 2018 19:00	NEWMARKET (JULY)	Little Jo	1	1.35	284.56	###############	###############	###############	118214803.01	############	###########
17 Aug 2018 19:45	CATTERICK	Loveisili	2	1.15	284.70	###############	###############	###############	51550098.02	############	###########
18 Aug 2018 13:50	NEWBURY	Boitron	1	1.60	285.27	###############	###############	###############	207746895.04	############	###########
18 Aug 2018 15:55	NEWMARKET (JULY)	Star Terms	1	1.46	285.72	###############	###############	###############	164050798.12	############	###########
18 Aug 2018 17:30	MARKET RASEN	Angel Of Harlem	1	1.22	285.92	###############	###############	###############	80263636.14	############	###########
18 Aug 2018 17:40	CHEPSTOW	The Establishmer	1	1.27	286.18	###############	###############	###############	99588930.71	############	###########
19 Aug 2018 16:25	SOUTHWELL	Sheelbewhatshe	2	1.45	286.61	###############	###############	###############	168222302.13	############	###########
19 Aug 2018 17:30	SOUTHWELL	King's Reste	2	1.15	286.75	###############	###############	###############	57335767.98	############	###########
20 Aug 2018 14:05	THIRSK	Topical	1	1.19	286.93	###############	###############	###############	73169995.90	############	###########
20 Aug 2018 14:35	THIRSK	Fuente	2	1.17	287.09	###############	###############	###############	66089836.03	############	###########
20 Aug 2018 15:05	THIRSK	Bedouin's Story	1	1.37	287.45	###############	###############	###############	145065246.27	############	###########
20 Aug 2018 16:35	THIRSK	Star Shield	3	1.22	287.66	###############	###############	###############	87850729.01	############	###########
21 Aug 2018 14:10	BRIGHTON	Stormy Road	1	1.26	287.90	###############	###############	###############	104965648.30	############	###########
21 Aug 2018 14:20	HAMILTON	Collide	1	1.09	287.98	###############	###############	###############	36806608.29	############	###########
21 Aug 2018 14:30	KEMPTON (A.W)	Ballet Red	2	1.41	288.37	###############	###############	###############	168429084.35	############	###########
21 Aug 2018 15:00	KEMPTON (A.W)	Enzemble	1	1.47	288.82	###############	###############	###############	197035326.52	############	###########
21 Aug 2018 15:10	BRIGHTON	Brexitmeansbrex	1	1.56	289.35	###############	###############	###############	240282484.57	############	###########
21 Aug 2018 15:40	BRIGHTON	Mamillius	3	1.64	288.35	###############	###############	###############	282297593.30	############	###########
21 Aug 2018 17:20	YARMOUTH	Queen Constanti	3	1.46	287.35	###############	###############	###############	209394239.83	############	###########
21 Aug 2018 17:50	YARMOUTH	Encryption	1	1.38	287.71	###############	###############	###############	176956340.85	############	###########
21 Aug 2018 18:20	YARMOUTH	Lunar Deity	2	1.77	288.44	###############	###############	###############	365382246.64	############	###########
21 Aug 2018 18:30	NEWTON ABBOT	Lord Topper	1	1.67	289.08	###############	###############	###############	330170312.08	############	###########
22 Aug 2018 14:15	BRIGHTON	King's Girl	2	1.09	289.16	###############	###############	###############	45837002.36	############	###########
22 Aug 2018 15:00	YORK	Cross Counter	2	1.37	289.52	###############	###############	###############	189288994.23	############	###########
22 Aug 2018 15:15	CARLISLE	Bugler Bob	3	1.25	289.75	###############	###############	###############	130264081.50	############	###########
22 Aug 2018 15:35	YORK	Poet's Word	2	1.39	290.12	###############	###############	###############	205752116.73	############	###########
22 Aug 2018 16:00	BRIGHTON	Fairlight	1	1.71	290.80	###############	###############	###############	381878566.50	############	###########
22 Aug 2018 16:35	BRIGHTON	Pour La Victoire	1	1.49	291.26	###############	###############	###############	272906021.48	############	###########
22 Aug 2018 17:45	KEMPTON (A.W)	Lively Lydia	1	1.18	291.43	###############	###############	###############	102707345.76	############	###########
22 Aug 2018 18:30	WORCESTER	Carntop	1	1.14	291.57	###############	###############	###############	80602442.56	############	###########
22 Aug 2018 20:15	KEMPTON (A.W)	Ortiz	1	1.64	292.18	###############	###############	###############	371047587.03	############	###########

THE HORSE RACING PLACE BET INVESTMENT STRATEGY

23 Aug 2018 14:35	STRATFORD	Go Another One	1	0.00	292.18	############	############	############	############	############	############
23 Aug 2018 14:50	CHEPSTOW	The Groove	1	1.23	292.39	############	############	############	130731660.15	############	############
23 Aug 2018 15:25	CHEPSTOW	K Club	2	1.13	292.52	############	############	############	74741563.70	############	############
23 Aug 2018 16:15	YORK	Lah Ti Dar	1	1.19	292.70	############	############	############	109947714.88	############	############
23 Aug 2018 17:15	FONTWELL	Walden Prince	2	1.59	293.26	############	############	############	344660045.89	############	############
23 Aug 2018 17:25	STRATFORD	Laughing Luis	1	1.17	293.42	############	############	############	102238437.17	############	############
23 Aug 2018 18:10	WOLVERHAMPTON (	Grenadier	3	1.12	293.53	############	############	############	72781739.22	############	############
23 Aug 2018 19:50	FONTWELL	Longhouse Sale	1	1.15	293.68	############	############	############	91523037.06	############	############
23 Aug 2018 20:40	WOLVERHAMPTON (	Rawdaa	2	1.01	293.69	############	############	############	6147297.32	############	############
24 Aug 2018 14:05	NEWMARKET (JULY)	Ice Gala	2	1.66	294.31	############	############	############	405924484.12	############	############
24 Aug 2018 14:15	FFOS LAS	Momkin	2	1.04	294.35	############	############	############	25413332.85	############	############
24 Aug 2018 14:25	YORK	Stradivarius	1	1.10	294.45	############	############	############	63660398.80	############	############
24 Aug 2018 15:00	YORK	Shine So Bright	3	1.61	295.03	############	############	############	390270074.84	############	############
24 Aug 2018 16:50	YORK	Crack On Crack O	2	2.11	296.08	############	############	############	731823567.96	############	############
24 Aug 2018 17:35	GOODWOOD	Fox Premier	2	1.72	296.77	############	############	############	501042016.85	############	############
24 Aug 2018 18:25	SALISBURY	Rosamour	2	1.71	297.44	############	############	############	511870091.55	############	############
24 Aug 2018 19:55	SALISBURY	Ravenous	1	1.46	297.88	############	############	############	343407155.93	############	############
25 Aug 2018 13:55	CHELMSFORD (A.W)	Sophosc	1	1.19	298.06	############	############	############	145104454.12	############	############
25 Aug 2018 16:15	YORK	Sabre	3	1.65	298.67	############	############	############	501125869.40	############	############
25 Aug 2018 16:40	CHELMSFORD (A.W)	Artarmon	1	1.37	299.02	############	############	############	294527092.70	############	############
26 Aug 2018 14:10	BEVERLEY	Withernsea	1	1.11	299.13	############	############	############	89182007.65	############	############
26 Aug 2018 15:15	BEVERLEY	Princess Power	2	1.59	299.69	############	############	############	480970728.44	############	############
26 Aug 2018 15:25	YARMOUTH	No Way Jose	3	1.69	300.35	############	############	############	579084681.02	############	############
26 Aug 2018 16:10	GOODWOOD	Dream Of Dream	2	1.31	300.64	############	############	############	269144292.44	############	############
26 Aug 2018 17:30	BEVERLEY	One Boy	1	1.67	301.28	############	############	############	590715288.42	############	############
26 Aug 2018 17:50	GOODWOOD	Geetanjali	3	2.01	300.28	############	############	############	920312377.74	############	############
27 Aug 2018 14:40	CARTMEL	Ormesher	1	1.11	300.38	############	############	############	105293759.22	############	############
27 Aug 2018 15:15	CARTMEL	Wells De Lune	1	1.40	300.76	############	############	############	384992272.34	############	############
27 Aug 2018 16:25	CARTMEL	Raise A Spark	2	2.32	302.01	############	############	############	############	############	############
27 Aug 2018 16:50	EPSOM	Bathsheba Bay	3	1.46	302.45	############	############	############	481401267.19	############	############
28 Aug 2018 13:55	RIPON	Golden Circle	1	1.12	302.56	############	############	############	128471346.87	############	############
28 Aug 2018 14:45	EPSOM	War Eagle	2	1.31	302.86	############	############	############	333875618.63	############	############
28 Aug 2018 15:00	RIPON	Iconic Choice	1	1.27	303.12	############	############	############	295302214.49	############	############
28 Aug 2018 16:35	RIPON	Give It Some Ted	1	1.54	303.63	############	############	############	598577588.78	############	############
28 Aug 2018 16:55	EPSOM	Fresh Terms	1	1.27	303.88	############	############	############	307369591.84	############	############
28 Aug 2018 18:10	STRATFORD	Guerrilla Tactics	1	1.53	304.39	############	############	############	611500418.90	############	############
28 Aug 2018 18:50	CHELMSFORD (A.W)	Dolcissimo	2	1.22	304.60	############	############	############	260556867.17	############	############
28 Aug 2018 19:20	CHELMSFORD (A.W)	Broughtons Story	3	1.85	303.60	############	############	############	############	############	############
29 Aug 2018 14:00	CATTERICK	Que Amoro	1	1.04	303.63	############	############	############	49930630.89	############	############
29 Aug 2018 14:10	MUSSELBURGH	Caballero	1	1.17	303.80	############	############	############	212629591.65	############	############
29 Aug 2018 14:50	LINGFIELD (A.W)	Chicago Doll	3	1.22	304.00	############	############	############	277506632.35	############	############
29 Aug 2018 15:00	CATTERICK	Romaana	1	1.06	304.06	############	############	############	76516146.90	############	############
29 Aug 2018 15:20	LINGFIELD (A.W)	Outback Travelle	3	1.19	304.24	############	############	############	243028035.25	############	############
29 Aug 2018 15:50	LINGFIELD (A.W)	Exchequer	2	1.41	304.63	############	############	############	529410992.89	############	############
29 Aug 2018 16:00	CATTERICK	Guardia Svizzera	1	1.23	304.85	############	############	############	303074880.97	############	############
29 Aug 2018 16:55	LINGFIELD	Zoffany Bay	2	1.18	305.02	############	############	############	239916711.21	############	############
29 Aug 2018 18:15	WORCESTER	Timeforben	2	2.00	305.97	############	############	############	############	############	############
29 Aug 2018 18:55	KEMPTON (A.W)	Maaward	1	1.10	306.07	############	############	############	141210977.60	############	############
29 Aug 2018 19:45	WORCESTER	David's Phoebe	2	1.83	306.86	############	############	############	############	############	############
29 Aug 2018 20:55	KEMPTON (A.W)	Chloellie	1	2.25	308.05	############	############	############	############	############	############
30 Aug 2018 14:00	CHELMSFORD (A.W)	Federal Law	2	1.04	308.09	############	############	############	62817800.47	############	############
30 Aug 2018 16:30	CHELMSFORD (A.W)	Lady Baker	1	1.21	308.29	############	############	############	330453039.37	############	############
30 Aug 2018 16:35	FONTWELL	Magical Thomas	1	1.25	308.52	############	############	############	397527138.44	############	############
30 Aug 2018 18:05	FONTWELL	Mercers Court	1	1.47	308.97	############	############	############	756692908.01	############	############
30 Aug 2018 19:05	FONTWELL	Brave Eagle	1	0.00	308.97	############	############	############	############	############	############
30 Aug 2018 19:50	SEDGEFIELD	Strong Team	2	2.13	310.04	############	############	############	############	############	############
31 Aug 2018 13:50	BANGOR-ON-DEE	Full Bore	1	1.30	310.32	############	############	############	496162587.88	############	############
31 Aug 2018 14:00	THIRSK	Never Do Nothin	1	1.10	310.42	############	############	############	167868342.23	############	############
31 Aug 2018 14:55	BANGOR-ON-DEE	Captain Peacock	1	1.15	310.56	############	############	############	253061525.92	############	############
31 Aug 2018 16:30	WOLVERHAMPTON (	Muthhila	1	1.13	310.68	############	############	############	220964889.05	############	############
31 Aug 2018 16:55	HAMILTON	Princes Des Sable	1	2.22	311.84	############	############	############	############	############	############
31 Aug 2018 17:05	WOLVERHAMPTON (	Theatre Of War	2	1.13	311.97	############	############	############	735967631.63	############	############
31 Aug 2018 17:45	NEWCASTLE (A.W)	[illegible]	1	[illegible]	311.31	############	############	############	657696243.43	############	############
31 Aug 2018 18:45	NEWCASTLE (A.W)	Spanish Archer	2	1.09	312.39	############	############	############	167383693.95	############	############
31 Aug 2018 20:00	HAMILTON	Guardia Svizzera	1	1.28	312.66	############	############	############	633092041.00	############	############
31 Aug 2018 20:15	NEWCASTLE (A.W)	Garrus	1	1.04	312.70	############	############	############	75773705.54	############	############
01 Sep 2018 13:55	NEWTON ABBOT	Leapaway	1	1.12	312.82	############	############	############	227775758.85	############	############
01 Sep 2018 14:10	BEVERLEY	Bertog	2	1.26	313.06	############	############	############	496475229.05	############	############
01 Sep 2018 15:15	CHESTER	Durotto	1	1.32	313.56	############	############	############	618990039.42	############	############
01 Sep 2018 16:30	BEVERLEY	Poet's Dawn	2	1.75	314.08	############	############	############	############	############	############
01 Sep 2018 17:05	BEVERLEY	Macho Mover	2	1.30	314.36	############	############	############	611697563.01	############	############
01 Sep 2018 17:10	WOLVERHAMPTON (	Fearsome	3	1.74	313.36	############	############	############	############	############	############
01 Sep 2018 17:40	WOLVERHAMPTON (	Liamba	2	1.46	313.80	############	############	############	987229503.60	############	############
01 Sep 2018 19:15	CHELMSFORD (A.W)	Fox Coach	1	1.49	314.27	############	############	############	############	############	############
02 Sep 2018 16:00	BRIGHTON	Double Reflectio	1	1.69	314.92	############	############	############	############	############	############
03 Sep 2018 14:30	BRIGHTON	Make A Wish	2	1.21	315.12	############	############	############	488649749.41	############	############
03 Sep 2018 15:30	BRIGHTON	Hameem	1	1.05	315.17	############	############	############	117566802.80	############	############
03 Sep 2018 16:25	WINDSOR	Golden Force	1	1.65	315.79	############	############	############	############	############	############
03 Sep 2018 16:30	BRIGHTON	De Vegas Kid	1	1.05	315.83	############	############	############	121691193.20	############	############
03 Sep 2018 18:50	NEWCASTLE (A.W)	Hard Taskmaster	1	1.22	316.05	############	############	############	536779853.22	############	############
03 Sep 2018 19:00	WINDSOR	Prabeni	2	1.04	316.08	############	############	############	98669896.66	############	############
04 Sep 2018 14:15	STRATFORD	Henry Smith	1	1.06	316.14	############	############	############	148300854.67	############	############
04 Sep 2018 15:40	GOODWOOD	Princess Power	1	1.40	316.52	############	############	############	991638381.59	############	############
04 Sep 2018 16:10	GOODWOOD	Austrian School	2	1.35	316.86	############	############	############	885037255.57	############	############
05 Sep 2018 14:10	LINGFIELD (A.W)	Meringue	1	1.14	316.99	############	############	############	360210163.02	############	############
05 Sep 2018 14:50	SOUTHWELL	Beat That	1	1.14	317.13	############	############	############	362731634.16	############	############
05 Sep 2018 16:10	LINGFIELD (A.W)	King Athelstan	2	1.28	317.39	############	############	############	730541511.19	############	############
06 Sep 2018 15:10	HAYDOCK	Waldstern	2	1.05	317.44	############	############	############	132280195.06	############	############
06 Sep 2018 15:30	SEDGEFIELD	High Expectation	1	1.44	317.86	############	############	############	############	############	############

THE HORSE RACING PLACE BET INVESTMENT STRATEGY

06 Sep 2018 18:10	CHELMSFORD (A.W)	Storm Shelter	1	1.72	318.54	###############	###############	###############	############	############	###########
06 Sep 2018 18:30	CARLISLE	Collide	1	1.08	318.62	###############	###############	###############	224651768.51	############	###########
06 Sep 2018 19:45	CHELMSFORD (A.W)	Saint Diana	2	1.22	318.82	###############	###############	###############	620263532.87	############	###########
07 Sep 2018 15:15	ASCOT	Sextant	2	0.00	317.82	###############	###############	###############	############	############	###########
07 Sep 2018 18:45	KEMPTON (A.W)	Alfurat River	2	1.27	318.08	###############	###############	###############	731125771.54	############	###########
08 Sep 2018 14:10	ASCOT	Model Guest	2	1.46	318.52	###############	###############	###############	############	############	###########
08 Sep 2018 14:20	STRATFORD	Competition	3	1.07	318.59	###############	###############	###############	196528597.68	############	###########
08 Sep 2018 14:40	KEMPTON (A.W)	Indian Sounds	1	1.57	319.13	###############	###############	###############	############	############	###########
08 Sep 2018 14:55	STRATFORD	Golden Birthday	1	0.00	319.13	###############	###############	###############	############	############	###########
08 Sep 2018 16:55	THIRSK	Blue Mist	2	1.17	319.29	###############	###############	###############	467974204.57	############	###########
09 Sep 2018 14:00	FONTWELL	Bold Image	3	1.40	318.29	###############	###############	###############	############	############	###########
09 Sep 2018 14:30	FONTWELL	Nordican Bleue	2	1.27	318.55	###############	###############	###############	764562216.19	############	###########
09 Sep 2018 14:55	YORK	Limato	1	1.28	318.82	###############	###############	###############	803583206.34	############	###########
09 Sep 2018 16:40	FONTWELL	Hardtorock	1	1.51	319.30	###############	###############	###############	############	############	###########
10 Sep 2018 14:20	NEWTON ABBOT	Leapaway	1	1.07	319.37	###############	###############	###############	208902905.55	############	###########
10 Sep 2018 14:55	NEWTON ABBOT	Roll The Dough	1	1.64	319.97	###############	###############	###############	############	############	###########
10 Sep 2018 16:40	BRIGHTON	Nyala	1	1.40	320.36	###############	###############	###############	############	############	###########
10 Sep 2018 17:25	PERTH	Carrie Des Cham	1	1.11	320.46	###############	###############	###############	346765890.33	############	###########
10 Sep 2018 18:15	CHELMSFORD (A.W)	Fognini	2	1.30	320.75	###############	###############	###############	950926643.80	############	###########
10 Sep 2018 20:45	CHELMSFORD (A.W)	Lyford	1	1.37	321.09	###############	###############	###############	############	############	###########
11 Sep 2018 14:40	LEICESTER	Naqaawa	1	1.40	321.47	###############	###############	###############	############	############	###########
11 Sep 2018 15:55	WORCESTER	Premier King	2	1.16	321.63	###############	###############	###############	534777333.27	############	###########
12 Sep 2018 16:50	CARLISLE	Just Hiss	3	1.90	322.48	###############	###############	###############	############	############	###########
12 Sep 2018 17:05	UTTOXETER	Strong Team	3	1.54	322.99	###############	###############	###############	############	############	###########
12 Sep 2018 18:15	KEMPTON (A.W)	Smart Illusion	3	1.51	323.48	###############	###############	###############	############	############	###########
12 Sep 2018 19:15	KEMPTON (A.W)	Quicksand	1	1.16	323.63	###############	###############	###############	593274828.03	############	###########
13 Sep 2018 15:00	DONCASTER	Pilaster	3	1.61	322.63	###############	###############	###############	############	############	###########
13 Sep 2018 15:25	FFOS LAS	Valentino Sunrise	1	2.03	323.61	###############	###############	###############	############	############	###########
13 Sep 2018 15:55	FFOS LAS	Fox Fearless	2	1.34	323.94	###############	###############	###############	############	############	###########
14 Sep 2018 14:00	CHESTER	Indomitable	1	1.19	324.12	###############	###############	###############	782579196.17	############	###########
14 Sep 2018 16:00	SALISBURY	Jash	1	1.04	324.16	###############	###############	###############	166318673.38	############	###########
14 Sep 2018 16:30	SANDOWN	Firmament	3	1.97	325.08	###############	###############	###############	############	############	###########
14 Sep 2018 16:35	SALISBURY	Jersey Wonder	1	1.46	325.52	###############	###############	###############	############	############	###########
14 Sep 2018 16:40	DONCASTER	Buffalo River	3	1.77	324.52	###############	###############	###############	############	############	###########
14 Sep 2018 17:45	DONCASTER	Jack Regan	1	1.83	325.32	###############	###############	###############	############	############	###########
14 Sep 2018 18:40	SALISBURY	Swift And Sure	1	1.19	325.50	###############	###############	###############	918358366.85	############	###########
14 Sep 2018 19:10	SALISBURY	Foxtrot Lady	1	1.07	325.56	###############	###############	###############	341556810.49	############	###########
15 Sep 2018 14:00	BATH	Rosamour	3	1.60	326.13	###############	###############	###############	############	############	###########
15 Sep 2018 14:55	MUSSELBURGH	Blame Roberta	1	1.14	326.27	###############	###############	###############	706069654.22	############	###########
15 Sep 2018 15:05	LINGFIELD (A.W)	Tabarrak	1	1.19	326.45	###############	###############	###############	964945049.58	############	###########
15 Sep 2018 16:00	CHELMSFORD (A.W)	Saint Diana	1	1.54	326.96	###############	###############	###############	############	############	###########
15 Sep 2018 17:10	CHELMSFORD (A.W)	Refrain	2	1.76	327.68	###############	###############	###############	############	############	###########
16 Sep 2018 15:20	BATH	Tigerwolf	2	1.53	328.19	###############	###############	###############	############	############	###########
16 Sep 2018 16:30	BATH	Bawaasil	1	1.12	328.31	###############	###############	###############	673229753.75	############	###########
17 Sep 2018 14:20	WORCESTER	Bermeo	1	2.34	329.58	###############	###############	###############	############	############	###########
17 Sep 2018 14:50	WORCESTER	Leoncavallo	2	1.10	329.67	###############	###############	###############	602205136.78	############	###########
17 Sep 2018 15:00	HEXHAM	Vivant	1	1.37	330.02	###############	###############	###############	############	############	###########
17 Sep 2018 15:20	WORCESTER	Theo	1	1.37	330.37	###############	###############	###############	############	############	###########
17 Sep 2018 16:10	BRIGHTON	Wiley Post	3	1.56	330.90	###############	###############	###############	############	############	###########
18 Sep 2018 13:50	YARMOUTH	Massam	1	1.20	331.09	###############	###############	###############	############	############	###########
18 Sep 2018 14:10	REDCAR	Harperelle	3	1.10	331.19	###############	###############	###############	651849103.51	############	###########
18 Sep 2018 14:20	YARMOUTH	Swindler	2	1.18	331.36	###############	###############	###############	############	############	###########
18 Sep 2018 15:00	LINGFIELD (A.W)	Wilbury Twist	2	1.11	331.46	###############	###############	###############	727104756.59	############	###########
18 Sep 2018 16:40	REDCAR	Field Gun	2	1.07	331.53	###############	###############	###############	465247893.57	############	###########
19 Sep 2018 14:40	SANDOWN	Good Fortune	2	1.32	331.83	###############	###############	###############	############	############	###########
19 Sep 2018 15:00	YARMOUTH	Sovereign Grant	3	1.28	332.10	###############	###############	###############	############	############	###########
19 Sep 2018 16:45	KELSO	Trongate	1	1.32	332.41	###############	###############	###############	############	############	###########
19 Sep 2018 16:55	SANDOWN	Geetanjali	1	1.54	332.92	###############	###############	###############	############	############	###########
19 Sep 2018 17:10	YARMOUTH	Encore D'Or	1	1.55	333.44	###############	###############	###############	############	############	###########
19 Sep 2018 18:45	KELSO	Auntie Mary	1	1.50	333.92	###############	###############	###############	############	############	###########
20 Sep 2018 13:30	AYR	Dark Jedi	2	1.24	334.15	###############	###############	###############	############	############	###########
20 Sep 2018 14:20	YARMOUTH	Boerhan	3	1.07	333.15	###############	###############	###############	534913816.09	############	###########
20 Sep 2018 16:55	PONTEFRACT	Baritone	1	0.00	333.15	###############	###############	###############	############	############	###########
20 Sep 2018 20:15	CHELMSFORD (A.W)	Satchville Flyer	3	1.54	333.66	###############	###############	###############	############	############	###########
21 Sep 2018 14:30	AYR	Lightning Attack	3	1.85	334.47	###############	###############	###############	############	############	###########
21 Sep 2018 14:40	NEWTON ABBOT	Scoop The Pot	2	1.98	335.40	###############	###############	###############	############	############	###########
21 Sep 2018 15:25	NEWBURY	Beat Le Bon	3	1.84	334.40	###############	###############	###############	############	############	###########
21 Sep 2018 15:45	NEWTON ABBOT	Rocket Ronnie	1	2.16	335.50	###############	###############	###############	############	############	###########
21 Sep 2018 16:45	AYR	Arrowtown	1	1.31	335.79	###############	###############	###############	############	############	###########
22 Sep 2018 14:50	CHELMSFORD (A.W)	Anasheed	1	1.20	335.98	###############	###############	###############	############	############	###########
22 Sep 2018 14:55	NEWBURY	Shine So Bright	3	1.85	336.79	###############	###############	###############	############	############	###########
22 Sep 2018 15:20	NEWMARKET	Amandine	2	1.72	337.47	###############	###############	###############	############	############	###########
22 Sep 2018 16:05	NEWBURY	Ballylemon	3	1.56	338.00	###############	###############	###############	############	############	###########
22 Sep 2018 16:35	CHELMSFORD (A.W)	Orin Swift	2	1.88	338.84	###############	###############	###############	############	############	###########
22 Sep 2018 17:05	CHELMSFORD (A.W)	Swordbill	1	1.21	339.04	###############	###############	###############	############	############	###########
22 Sep 2018 19:45	WOLVERHAMPTON	Daily Trader	2	2.03	340.02	###############	###############	###############	############	############	###########
23 Sep 2018 14:20	PLUMPTON	Ilewin Geez	2	1.24	340.25	###############	###############	###############	############	############	###########
23 Sep 2018 15:35	HAMILTON	Jamil	1	1.06	340.30	###############	###############	###############	691847269.31	############	###########
23 Sep 2018 17:00	PLUMPTON	Eric The Third	1	1.55	340.83	###############	###############	###############	############	############	###########
24 Sep 2018 13:30	HAMILTON	Happy Power	3	1.34	341.15	###############	###############	###############	############	############	###########
24 Sep 2018 14:50	LEICESTER	Faro Angel	1	1.22	341.36	###############	###############	###############	############	############	###########
24 Sep 2018 15:40	KEMPTON (A.W)	Alexa Rose	1	1.17	341.52	###############	###############	###############	############	############	###########
24 Sep 2018 16:20	LEICESTER	Outbox	1	1.12	341.63	###############	###############	###############	############	############	###########
24 Sep 2018 19:00	NEWCASTLE (A.W)	Turgenev	1	1.16	341.79	###############	###############	###############	############	############	###########
24 Sep 2018 19:30	NEWCASTLE (A.W)	My Ukulele	1	1.77	342.52	###############	###############	###############	############	############	###########
25 Sep 2018 14:35	LINGFIELD (A.W)	Sam Cooke	2	1.09	342.60	###############	###############	###############	############	############	###########
25 Sep 2018 14:45	BEVERLEY	Sameem	1	1.41	342.99	###############	###############	###############	############	############	###########
25 Sep 2018 15:45	LINGFIELD (A.W)	Welsh Lord	2	1.09	343.07	###############	###############	###############	############	############	###########
25 Sep 2018 16:30	BEVERLEY	Detachment	1	1.18	343.25	###############	###############	###############	############	############	###########

THE HORSE RACING PLACE BET INVESTMENT STRATEGY

Date	Course	Horse		Odds	Bank
26 Sep 2018 14:00	GOODWOOD	Pablo Escobarr	1	1.13	343.37
26 Sep 2018 14:10	PERTH	Brandy James	2	1.24	343.59
26 Sep 2018 15:45	PERTH	Jaunty Thor	2	1.24	343.82
27 Sep 2018 16:00	PERTH	Global Jackpot	1	1.13	343.94
27 Sep 2018 17:00	PONTEFRACT	Never Do Nothin	1	1.35	344.28
27 Sep 2018 19:15	KEMPTON (A.W)	Buffalo River	2	1.05	344.33
28 Sep 2018 14:40	HAYDOCK	Lady Aria	1	1.06	344.38
28 Sep 2018 15:00	NEWMARKET	Main Edition	3	1.45	344.81
28 Sep 2018 15:15	HAYDOCK	Wise Counsel	1	1.11	344.91
29 Sep 2018 13:30	HAYDOCK	Chartered	2	1.58	345.46
29 Sep 2018 13:40	MARKET RASEN	King's Reste	2	1.19	345.65
29 Sep 2018 13:55	RIPON	Fastman	1	1.21	345.84
29 Sep 2018 14:30	RIPON	Riviera Nights	1	2.00	346.79
29 Sep 2018 14:35	CHESTER	Intransigent	2	1.62	347.38
29 Sep 2018 14:40	HAYDOCK	Cap Francais	1	1.76	348.10
29 Sep 2018 16:10	RIPON	Multellie	1	1.26	348.35
30 Sep 2018 14:10	MUSSELBURGH	Nate The Great	1	1.07	348.42
30 Sep 2018 17:25	MUSSELBURGH	Our Place In Loui	1	1.74	349.12
01 Oct 2018 14:55	NEWTON ABBOT	Risk And Roll	2	0.00	348.12
01 Oct 2018 15:05	CATTERICK	Sharja Silk	1	1.12	348.24
02 Oct 2018 15:05	SEDGEFIELD	Caid du Lin	2	1.06	348.30
02 Oct 2018 15:35	SEDGEFIELD	Beach Break	3	1.78	347.30
02 Oct 2018 16:00	SOUTHWELL	Itchy Feet	1	1.11	347.40
02 Oct 2018 16:55	AYR	Daawy	1	1.31	347.69
03 Oct 2018 14:00	NOTTINGHAM	Ambling	2	1.29	347.97
03 Oct 2018 16:20	SALISBURY	Blackheath	2	2.08	349.00
04 Oct 2018 13:30	HUNTINGDON	Nordican Bleue	1	1.11	349.10
04 Oct 2018 14:10	WARWICK	Lissycasey	3	1.36	348.10
04 Oct 2018 14:45	WARWICK	Pontresina	2	1.38	348.46
04 Oct 2018 14:55	LINGFIELD (A.W)	Gaudi	1	1.06	348.52
04 Oct 2018 16:20	HUNTINGDON	Tempichinis	1	1.24	348.74
04 Oct 2018 18:15	CHELMSFORD (A.W)	Accommodate	1	1.58	349.30
04 Oct 2018 18:45	CHELMSFORD (A.W)	Alimankind	1	1.14	349.43
05 Oct 2018 14:15	HEXHAM	Mac Tottie	1	1.11	349.53
05 Oct 2018 15:35	ASCOT	Ghostwatch	1	1.46	349.97
05 Oct 2018 16:35	HEXHAM	Jaunty Thor	1	1.14	350.11
05 Oct 2018 17:00	FONTWELL	Mercers Court	1	1.64	350.72
06 Oct 2018 14:25	ASCOT	First Eleven	3	1.55	349.72
06 Oct 2018 14:40	NEWMARKET	Turgenev	1	1.23	349.93
06 Oct 2018 17:05	FONTWELL	Earth Moor	1	1.58	350.48
06 Oct 2018 17:45	WOLVERHAMPTON	Muneyra	1	1.07	350.55
07 Oct 2018 14:20	KELSO	Rocky's Treasure	1	0.00	350.55
07 Oct 2018 14:50	KELSO	Strong Team	2	1.70	351.21
07 Oct 2018 15:00	UTTOXETER	Anytime Will Do	1	1.23	351.43
07 Oct 2018 17:05	UTTOXETER	Polished Rock	1	1.47	351.88
08 Oct 2018 13:25	WINDSOR	Aspire Tower	3	1.80	352.64
08 Oct 2018 14:25	WINDSOR	Surrey Thunder	1	1.17	352.80
08 Oct 2018 14:50	STRATFORD	Jenkins	1	0.00	352.80
08 Oct 2018 16:25	STRATFORD	Lungarno Palace	1	1.10	352.90
08 Oct 2018 17:30	STRATFORD	Flash The Steel	3	1.25	353.14
08 Oct 2018 18:45	KEMPTON (A.W)	Cool Reflection	1	1.32	353.44
09 Oct 2018 13:50	BRIGHTON	Water Diviner	2	1.16	353.59
09 Oct 2018 15:50	LEICESTER	Huge Future	3	1.27	352.59
09 Oct 2018 16:55	LEICESTER	Compas Scoobie	2	1.85	353.40
09 Oct 2018 17:05	BRIGHTON	Kirkland Forever	1	1.42	353.80
10 Oct 2018 14:30	NOTTINGHAM	Alnadir	1	1.35	354.13
10 Oct 2018 16:10	LUDLOW	Sumkindofking	1	1.29	354.40
10 Oct 2018 17:40	KEMPTON (A.W)	Buffalo River	1	1.23	354.62
10 Oct 2018 20:40	KEMPTON (A.W)	Duke Cosimo	1	1.73	355.32
11 Oct 2018 13:25	WORCESTER	Kalahari Queen	1	1.42	355.72
11 Oct 2018 13:35	AYR	Epona	1	1.26	355.96
11 Oct 2018 14:35	AYR	Hot Hand	3	1.51	356.44
11 Oct 2018 15:10	AYR	Wjimbuta Legal	2	1.62	357.32
11 Oct 2018 15:30	WORCESTER	Winter Spice	1	1.67	357.95
11 Oct 2018 16:00	WORCESTER	Bradford Bridge	1	1.52	358.45
11 Oct 2018 17:45	CHELMSFORD (A.W)	Collect Call	2	1.28	358.72
12 Oct 2018 17:00	YORK	Sam Cooke	1	1.58	359.26
12 Oct 2018 19:45	WOLVERHAMPTON	Jersey Wonder	1	1.41	359.65
13 Oct 2018 14:40	YORK	Dave Dexter	1	1.63	360.25
13 Oct 2018 15:00	NEWMARKET	Too Darn Hot	1	1.45	360.68
13 Oct 2018 16:25	YORK	Jonah Jones	1	1.22	360.89
13 Oct 2018 17:45	CHELMSFORD (A.W)	El Gumryah	2	1.14	361.02
13 Oct 2018 20:45	CHELMSFORD (A.W)	Yaa Mous	1	1.75	361.74
15 Oct 2018 15:00	YARMOUTH	Reloaded	3	1.65	362.36
15 Oct 2018 19:15	KEMPTON (A.W)	Desert Friend	1	1.22	362.57
15 Oct 2018 19:45	KEMPTON (A.W)	Jahbath	1	1.07	362.63
15 Oct 2018 20:45	KEMPTON (A.W)	Rose Berry	2	2.06	363.64
16 Oct 2018 14:00	LEICESTER	Global Heat	3	1.31	363.94
16 Oct 2018 15:25	HEREFORD	Cresswell Legend	1	1.36	364.28
16 Oct 2018 15:35	LEICESTER	Estihdaaf	1	1.13	364.40
16 Oct 2018 15:55	HEREFORD	Marble Moon	1	1.24	364.63
16 Oct 2018 16:30	HEREFORD	Atlanta Ablaze	1	1.42	365.03
16 Oct 2018 17:00	HEREFORD	What's Occurring	1	1.30	365.31
17 Oct 2018 13:50	BATH	West End Charm	1	1.26	365.56
17 Oct 2018 14:20	NOTTINGHAM	Durell	2	1.34	365.88
17 Oct 2018 17:25	WETHERBY	Midnight Shadow	1	1.45	366.31
18 Oct 2018 14:20	UTTOXETER	Kublai	2	1.69	366.96
18 Oct 2018 14:30	BRIGHTON	Napanook	1	1.44	367.38
18 Oct 2018 15:15	CARLISLE	Al Dancer	1	1.12	367.49

51

THE HORSE RACING PLACE BET INVESTMENT STRATEGY

Date	Course	Horse	Pos	Odds	Running
18 Oct 2018 19:30	WOLVERHAMPTON	Repaupo	2	1.04	367.53
18 Oct 2018 20:15	CHELMSFORD (A.W)	Muneyra	2	1.11	367.64
19 Oct 2018 14:05	FAKENHAM	Collodi	1	1.39	368.02
19 Oct 2018 14:15	REDCAR	Absolute Dream	1	1.33	368.33
19 Oct 2018 14:20	WINCANTON	Marettimo	2	1.38	368.69
19 Oct 2018 14:30	HAYDOCK	Welcoming	1	1.33	369.00
19 Oct 2018 15:20	REDCAR	Barys	3	1.34	369.33
19 Oct 2018 16:30	WINCANTON	Beau Sancy	1	1.42	369.73
19 Oct 2018 16:40	HAYDOCK	New Graduate	2	1.43	370.13
19 Oct 2018 18:15	NEWCASTLE (A.W)	Boston George	1	1.20	370.32
20 Oct 2018 13:25	ASCOT	Stradivarius	1	1.39	370.69
20 Oct 2018 14:25	CATTERICK	Ice Gala	1	1.08	370.77
20 Oct 2018 14:40	ASCOT	Lah Ti Dar	3	1.28	371.03
21 Oct 2018 15:20	SEDGEFIELD	Absolutely Dylan	1	1.20	371.23
21 Oct 2018 17:15	KEMPTON	Admiral Barratry	2	1.32	371.53
22 Oct 2018 14:30	PONTEFRACT	Shallow Hal	1	1.04	371.56
22 Oct 2018 15:30	PONTEFRACT	Manuela De Vega	1	1.25	371.80
22 Oct 2018 18:40	KEMPTON (A.W)	Desirous	1	1.13	371.92
23 Oct 2018 14:20	EXETER	Beau Du Brizais	2	0.00	370.92
23 Oct 2018 14:30	YARMOUTH	Maqsad	3	1.10	371.02
23 Oct 2018 14:40	NEWCASTLE (A.W)	Turjomaan	1	1.10	371.11
23 Oct 2018 14:50	EXETER	Bradford Bridge	1	1.32	371.42
23 Oct 2018 15:50	EXETER	Earth Moor	1	1.11	371.52
24 Oct 2018 13:50	WORCESTER	Marienstar	1	1.51	372.00
24 Oct 2018 17:10	FONTWELL	Crackle Lyn Rosie	3	1.68	372.65
24 Oct 2018 17:20	WORCESTER	Oscar Rose	1	1.14	372.78
24 Oct 2018 17:25	CHELMSFORD (A.W)	So Hi Storm	1	1.33	373.10
24 Oct 2018 19:45	NEWCASTLE (A.W)	Ideological	2	1.19	373.28
24 Oct 2018 20:45	NEWCASTLE (A.W)	Ring Dancer	1	1.23	373.50
25 Oct 2018 15:20	LUDLOW	Pique Rock	1	1.14	373.63
25 Oct 2018 15:50	LUDLOW	Hoke Colburn	1	1.62	374.22
25 Oct 2018 16:10	CARLISLE	Zabeel Star	2	1.14	374.35
25 Oct 2018 16:35	SOUTHWELL	Royal Ruby	3	1.30	374.64
25 Oct 2018 17:15	CHELMSFORD (A.W)	Calling The Wind	1	1.30	374.93
25 Oct 2018 18:15	CHELMSFORD (A.W)	Fragrant Dawn	3	1.10	373.93
26 Oct 2018 15:45	CHELTENHAM	Lil Rockerfeller	1	1.45	374.35
26 Oct 2018 17:30	CHELTENHAM	Magic Dancer	2	2.14	375.44
27 Oct 2018 13:50	KELSO	Goldencard	1	1.22	375.65
27 Oct 2018 14:15	DONCASTER	Beat Le Bon	2	1.68	376.29
27 Oct 2018 14:20	NEWBURY	Young Rascal	1	1.26	376.54
27 Oct 2018 16:05	DONCASTER	Magna Grecia	1	1.73	377.23
27 Oct 2018 16:55	CHELTENHAM	Monbeg Legend	2	1.46	377.67
28 Oct 2018 12:40	AINTREE	Aye Aye Charlie	2	1.18	377.84
28 Oct 2018 13:15	AINTREE	Ready And Able	1	2.00	378.79
28 Oct 2018 13:35	WINCANTON	Pontresina	2	1.19	378.97
28 Oct 2018 14:10	WINCANTON	Eric The Third	1	0.00	378.97
29 Oct 2018 12:05	REDCAR	Finoah	2	1.17	379.13
29 Oct 2018 12:45	LEICESTER	Don Logan	2	1.52	379.63
29 Oct 2018 16:45	CHELMSFORD (A.W)	Say The Word	2	1.30	379.91
30 Oct 2018 13:05	BANGOR-ON-DEE	Anytime Will Do	1	1.24	380.14
30 Oct 2018 19:15	WOLVERHAMPTON	Coastline	2	1.11	380.25
31 Oct 2018 13:10	NOTTINGHAM	Mubariz	1	1.29	380.52
31 Oct 2018 16:00	FAKENHAM	Skandiburg	1	1.20	380.71
31 Oct 2018 17:15	KEMPTON (A.W)	Ticklish	3	1.26	380.96
01 Nov 2018 13:30	LINGFIELD (A.W)	Alexa Rose	3	1.21	381.16
01 Nov 2018 13:40	STRATFORD	Stowaway Magic	1	1.06	381.21
01 Nov 2018 16:10	LINGFIELD (A.W)	Garth Rockett	1	1.48	381.67
01 Nov 2018 20:15	WOLVERHAMPTON	Calvinist	2	1.72	382.35
02 Nov 2018 13:30	UTTOXETER	Queen's Magic	2	1.18	382.52
02 Nov 2018 14:40	UTTOXETER	Claimantakinforg	1	0.00	382.52
02 Nov 2018 16:10	WETHERBY	Denmead	3	1.12	382.64
03 Nov 2018 12:40	ASCOT	Pym	2	1.25	382.87
03 Nov 2018 12:50	NEWMARKET	Imperial Charm	1	1.21	383.07
03 Nov 2018 13:25	NEWMARKET	Aspire Tower	1	1.59	383.63
03 Nov 2018 15:30	NEWCASTLE (A.W)	Oscar's Ridge	3	1.08	383.71
03 Nov 2018 16:00	NEWCASTLE (A.W)	Frederickbarbaro	1	1.35	384.05
03 Nov 2018 16:30	NEWCASTLE (A.W)	You Never Can Te	1	1.19	384.23
03 Nov 2018 17:00	NEWCASTLE (A.W)	Deputise	1	1.35	384.60
04 Nov 2018 14:20	HUNTINGDON	Full Bore	1	1.17	384.72
04 Nov 2018 14:40	CARLISLE	Looksnowtlikebri	1	2.00	385.67
05 Nov 2018 13:30	PLUMPTON	Marettimo	2	1.30	385.96
05 Nov 2018 17:00	KEMPTON (A.W)	Cloudlam	3	1.13	386.08
05 Nov 2018 17:30	KEMPTON (A.W)	Salute The Soldie	1	1.36	386.43
06 Nov 2018 12:05	WOLVERHAMPTON	Leodis Dream	1	1.09	386.51
06 Nov 2018 13:00	EXETER	Cotswold Way	1	1.15	386.65
06 Nov 2018 13:45	WOLVERHAMPTON	Lord Murphy	2	1.72	387.34
06 Nov 2018 13:55	REDCAR	Parys Mountain	1	1.48	387.79
06 Nov 2018 14:05	EXETER	Ozzie The Oscar	1	1.88	388.63
06 Nov 2018 14:40	EXETER	Coup De Pinceau	1	0.00	388.63
06 Nov 2018 15:55	WOLVERHAMPTON	Eden Rose	2	1.42	389.02
06 Nov 2018 17:30	KEMPTON (A.W)	Nivaldo	1	1.28	389.28
07 Nov 2018 13:05	NOTTINGHAM	Private Secretary	2	1.21	389.48
07 Nov 2018 14:00	CHEPSTOW	Our Reward	3	1.59	390.04
07 Nov 2018 15:20	NOTTINGHAM	Honey Gg	1	1.97	390.96
07 Nov 2018 15:40	CHEPSTOW	Kateson	1	1.51	391.45
07 Nov 2018 16:00	NEWCASTLE (A.W)	Young John	1	1.15	391.59
07 Nov 2018 17:10	NEWCASTLE (A.W)	Solid Stone	1	1.11	391.69
07 Nov 2018 17:20	CHELMSFORD (A.W)	Flarepath	1	1.18	391.86
07 Nov 2018 18:10	NEWCASTLE (A.W)	Merweb	2	1.04	391.90

THE HORSE RACING PLACE BET INVESTMENT STRATEGY

Date	Course	Horse	Pos	Price	Bank
08 Nov 2018 12:55	MARKET RASEN	Idilico	2	1.26	392.15
08 Nov 2018 14:15	SEDGEFIELD	Informateur	1	1.12	392.26
08 Nov 2018 14:25	NEWBURY	Posh Trish	2	1.31	392.56
08 Nov 2018 14:35	MARKET RASEN	The Two Amigos	2	1.49	393.02
08 Nov 2018 15:50	SEDGEFIELD	I'm To Blame	1	1.15	393.16
08 Nov 2018 17:45	CHELMSFORD (A.W)	Uncle Jerry	1	1.64	393.77
08 Nov 2018 18:15	CHELMSFORD (A.W)	Brasca	1	1.15	393.92
09 Nov 2018 13:40	HEXHAM	Weather Front	1	1.11	394.02
09 Nov 2018 14:00	WARWICK	Kalashnikov	1	1.13	394.14
09 Nov 2018 14:10	HEXHAM	Militarian	2	2.24	395.32
09 Nov 2018 14:55	FONTWELL	Mon Port	2	1.13	395.45
09 Nov 2018 16:05	WARWICK	Eleanorofaquitaine	2	1.82	396.23
09 Nov 2018 18:45	NEWCASTLE (A.W)	Island Of Life	1	1.46	396.62
10 Nov 2018 11:50	KELSO	Aye Aye Charlie	1	1.05	396.71
10 Nov 2018 12:15	KELSO	Cool Mix	2	1.32	397.01
10 Nov 2018 12:20	DONCASTER	Dazzling Dan	1	1.64	397.62
10 Nov 2018 12:25	AINTREE	Robin Waters	2	0.00	396.62
10 Nov 2018 13:20	KELSO	Shanroe In Milan	3	1.97	395.62
10 Nov 2018 14:05	DONCASTER	Donjuan Triumphant	1	1.53	396.13
10 Nov 2018 15:00	WINCANTON	We Have A Dream	3	1.69	395.13
11 Nov 2018 13:25	FFOS LAS	Good Boy Bobby	3	1.14	395.26
11 Nov 2018 13:50	SANDOWN	Sevarano	2	1.27	395.52
11 Nov 2018 14:30	FFOS LAS	Acey Milan	2	1.15	395.66
12 Nov 2018 12:55	CARLISLE	Clondaw Anchor	1	1.07	395.73
12 Nov 2018 13:30	CARLISLE	Vinndication	1	1.20	395.92
12 Nov 2018 15:50	SOUTHWELL (A.W)	Point Zero	2	1.23	396.13
13 Nov 2018 14:40	HUNTINGDON	Mercers Court	2	2.16	397.23
13 Nov 2018 16:45	CHELMSFORD (A.W)	Mujassam	1	1.16	397.39
14 Nov 2018 14:35	EXETER	Just A Sting	1	1.60	397.96
14 Nov 2018 15:40	EXETER	Trans Express	2	1.55	398.48
14 Nov 2018 17:00	KEMPTON (A.W)	Lady Adelaide	1	2.30	399.71
15 Nov 2018 13:05	TAUNTON	Georgina Joy	2	1.12	399.83
15 Nov 2018 13:10	SOUTHWELL (A.W)	Theatre Of War	2	1.68	400.17
15 Nov 2018 14:25	LUDLOW	Samarquand	1	1.17	400.63
15 Nov 2018 14:35	TAUNTON	Misty Bloom	1	1.14	400.77
15 Nov 2018 15:30	LUDLOW	Elysees	1	1.17	400.93
15 Nov 2018 15:40	TAUNTON	Night Of Sin	1	0.00	400.93
15 Nov 2018 17:00	KEMPTON (A.W)	Fearlessly	3	1.24	401.16
15 Nov 2018 17:15	CHELMSFORD (A.W)	California Love	1	1.30	401.44
15 Nov 2018 17:45	CHELMSFORD (A.W)	Nananita	2	1.78	402.18
16 Nov 2018 12:00	NEWCASTLE	Weather Front	1	1.05	402.23
16 Nov 2018 12:40	CHELTENHAM	Station Master	2	1.97	403.15
16 Nov 2018 13:05	NEWCASTLE	Kovera	1	1.43	403.56
16 Nov 2018 14:00	LINGFIELD (A.W)	Uncle Jerry	2	1.13	403.68
16 Nov 2018 19:15	WOLVERHAMPTON	Coolagh Forest	1	1.36	404.03
17 Nov 2018 13:00	LINGFIELD (A.W)	Humanitarian	1	1.12	404.14
17 Nov 2018 13:05	WETHERBY	Miles To Milan	1	1.80	404.90
17 Nov 2018 14:00	UTTOXETER	Tokay Dokey	1	1.16	405.05
17 Nov 2018 14:15	WETHERBY	Cracking Find	2	1.61	405.63
17 Nov 2018 14:50	WETHERBY	Kajaki	1	1.45	406.06
17 Nov 2018 18:45	WOLVERHAMPTON	Magic Illusion	3	1.13	406.18
19 Nov 2018 14:00	PLUMPTON	Winter Spice	1	1.52	406.68
19 Nov 2018 14:15	HEREFORD	Renwick	1	1.18	406.85
19 Nov 2018 15:05	PLUMPTON	Bermeo	2	1.50	407.33
19 Nov 2018 15:20	HEREFORD	Love The Leader	1	1.37	407.68
19 Nov 2018 15:35	PLUMPTON	Welluptoscratch	3	1.35	408.02
20 Nov 2018 14:30	FAKENHAM	Theclockisticking	1	0.00	408.02
20 Nov 2018 15:00	FAKENHAM	Ontopoftheworld	1	0.00	408.02
21 Nov 2018 14:05	WARWICK	Pacific De Baune	1	0.00	408.02
21 Nov 2018 14:35	WARWICK	Erick Le Rouge	1	1.32	408.32
21 Nov 2018 16:10	KEMPTON (A.W)	Go Fox	3	2.08	409.35
21 Nov 2018 17:10	KEMPTON (A.W)	Headman	2	1.09	409.43
21 Nov 2018 17:40	KEMPTON (A.W)	Deference	1	1.26	409.71
21 Nov 2018 18:30	WOLVERHAMPTON	Earl Of Bunnacurry	1	1.34	410.10
22 Nov 2018 13:45	WINCANTON	Capeland	1	0.00	410.10
22 Nov 2018 14:15	WINCANTON	Rhythm Is A Dancer	1	1.05	410.15
22 Nov 2018 18:00	WOLVERHAMPTON	Cantiniere	1	1.10	410.24
22 Nov 2018 18:30	WOLVERHAMPTON	Finoah	3	1.56	409.24
23 Nov 2018 12:15	CATTERICK	Je Suis Charlie	1	1.19	409.42
23 Nov 2018 12:45	CATTERICK	Grow Nasa Grow	1	1.23	409.64
23 Nov 2018 14:05	ASCOT	Thomas Darby	2	1.38	410.01
23 Nov 2018 14:15	FFOS LAS	Sir Egbert	2	1.69	410.66
23 Nov 2018 18:15	KEMPTON (A.W)	Inhale	1	1.36	411.00
23 Nov 2018 18:45	KEMPTON (A.W)	Aquanura	3	1.36	410.00
24 Nov 2018 12:10	HAYDOCK	Grand Sancy	1	1.36	410.34
24 Nov 2018 14:00	LINGFIELD (A.W)	Red Impression	1	1.08	410.42
24 Nov 2018 14:05	ASCOT	Pullulugue	1	1.49	410.88
25 Nov 2018 14:20	EXETER	Lil Rockerfeller	1	1.18	411.05
26 Nov 2018 14:45	LUDLOW	Burn Baby Byrne	1	1.49	411.52
26 Nov 2018 15:00	MUSSELBURGH	Cap St Vincent	1	1.54	412.03
26 Nov 2018 15:30	MUSSELBURGH	All Hail Caesar	2	1.31	412.33
27 Nov 2018 12:40	SOUTHWELL (A.W)	Princess Harley	1	1.29	412.60
27 Nov 2018 13:00	LINGFIELD	Clondaw Anchor	3	1.35	412.94
27 Nov 2018 15:00	LINGFIELD	Duhallow Gesture	2	1.13	413.06
27 Nov 2018 15:20	SEDGEFIELD	Speedy Cargo	2	1.53	413.56
28 Nov 2018 14:45	WOLVERHAMPTON	Frisella	3	1.36	413.90
28 Nov 2018 15:55	WOLVERHAMPTON	Heavenly Holly	1	1.08	413.98
28 Nov 2018 16:15	NEWCASTLE (A.W)	Fabiolla	3	1.15	414.12
28 Nov 2018 17:45	NEWCASTLE (A.W)	False Id	1	2.28	415.34

THE HORSE RACING PLACE BET INVESTMENT STRATEGY

Date	Course	Horse	Pos	Odds	Bank
29 Nov 2018 12:05	WARWICK	Nestor Park	1	1.38	415.70
29 Nov 2018 15:30	AYR	Vinnie Lewis	2	1.10	415.79
29 Nov 2018 18:00	KEMPTON (A.W)	Manorah	1	1.47	416.24
29 Nov 2018 18:45	CHELMSFORD (A.W)	Valley Belle	2	1.59	416.80
30 Nov 2018 11:20	SOUTHWELL (A.W)	Honey Gg	1	1.75	417.52
30 Nov 2018 13:20	NEWBURY	Kateson	1	1.28	417.78
30 Nov 2018 17:45	NEWCASTLE (A.W)	Fightwithme	2	1.11	417.89
01 Dec 2018 12:00	DONCASTER	Anemoi	1	1.08	417.96
01 Dec 2018 12:35	DONCASTER	Rubenesque	1	0.00	417.96
01 Dec 2018 12:45	NEWBURY	Santini	1	1.64	418.57
01 Dec 2018 14:00	BANGOR-ON-DEE	Shantaluze	1	1.35	418.91
02 Dec 2018 13:45	LEICESTER	Trans Express	1	1.55	419.43
03 Dec 2018 13:00	PLUMPTON	Kalashnikov	1	1.13	419.56
03 Dec 2018 13:30	PLUMPTON	Royal Claret	1	1.30	419.84
04 Dec 2018 13:30	SOUTHWELL	Commodore Barry	1	1.10	419.94
04 Dec 2018 13:40	FAKENHAM	Skandiburg	1	1.25	420.18
04 Dec 2018 14:10	FAKENHAM	Song For Someone	2	1.20	420.37
04 Dec 2018 14:30	SOUTHWELL	Rouge Vif	1	1.39	420.74
04 Dec 2018 15:30	SOUTHWELL	Daario Naharis	2	1.39	421.11
05 Dec 2018 13:10	LUDLOW	Mystic Sky	2	1.52	421.61
05 Dec 2018 13:35	LINGFIELD (A.W)	Cantiniere	1	1.05	421.65
05 Dec 2018 13:55	HAYDOCK	The Big Bite	1	1.19	421.83
05 Dec 2018 19:15	NEWCASTLE (A.W)	Nick Vedder	2	1.32	422.14
06 Dec 2018 12:50	MARKET RASEN	General Custard	1	1.37	422.49
06 Dec 2018 13:55	MARKET RASEN	Pookie Pekan	1	1.22	422.70
07 Dec 2018 12:10	SEDGEFIELD	Millie The Minx	1	1.26	422.95
07 Dec 2018 14:50	SEDGEFIELD	Schiehallion Munro	1	1.38	423.31
08 Dec 2018 12:55	CHEPSTOW	Trixster	1	1.62	423.90
08 Dec 2018 13:50	SANDOWN	Lalor	3	1.41	422.90
08 Dec 2018 14:05	AINTREE	Definitly Red	1	1.23	423.12
08 Dec 2018 15:40	CHEPSTOW	Young Bull	1	1.52	423.62
08 Dec 2018 17:45	WOLVERHAMPTON	Fields Of Athenry	3	1.34	423.94
09 Dec 2018 12:00	KELSO	Romeo Brown	1	1.27	424.19
09 Dec 2018 12:30	KELSO	Donna's Diamond	1	1.23	424.41
09 Dec 2018 13:05	KELSO	Calett Mad	2	1.72	425.09
09 Dec 2018 13:35	KELSO	Xpo Universel	1	1.51	425.57
09 Dec 2018 14:25	HUNTINGDON	Charbel	1	1.43	425.98
10 Dec 2018 12:15	MUSSELBURGH	Golden Jeffrey	1	1.73	426.67
10 Dec 2018 13:00	LINGFIELD	Coded Message	1	1.39	427.04
10 Dec 2018 13:15	MUSSELBURGH	Wolfcatcher	1	0.00	427.04
10 Dec 2018 13:45	MUSSELBURGH	Ontopoftheworld	2	1.73	427.74
10 Dec 2018 14:15	MUSSELBURGH	Liva	1	1.44	428.16
10 Dec 2018 17:00	WOLVERHAMPTON	She's Got You	1	1.14	428.29
11 Dec 2018 12:30	UTTOXETER	Stop Talking	1	1.26	428.54
11 Dec 2018 13:10	FONTWELL	The Ogle Gogle Man	1	1.57	429.08
11 Dec 2018 13:40	FONTWELL	Tazka	1	1.30	429.36
11 Dec 2018 13:50	SOUTHWELL (A.W)	Honey Gg	2	1.56	429.89
11 Dec 2018 14:10	FONTWELL	Scoop The Pot	1	0.00	429.89
11 Dec 2018 14:40	FONTWELL	Outofthisworld	2	1.11	430.00
12 Dec 2018 13:20	HEXHAM	Derriana Spirit	1	1.15	430.14
12 Dec 2018 13:40	LINGFIELD (A.W)	Mainsail Atlantic	1	1.09	430.23
12 Dec 2018 13:50	HEXHAM	Inchcolm	1	1.64	430.84
13 Dec 2018 12:35	TAUNTON	Southfield Stone	1	1.07	430.90
13 Dec 2018 13:25	WARWICK	Jester Jet	2	1.30	431.19
13 Dec 2018 20:45	CHELMSFORD (A.W)	Your Band	2	1.27	431.45
14 Dec 2018 12:10	CHELTENHAM	Elixir De Nutz	1	1.28	431.71
14 Dec 2018 12:25	BANGOR-ON-DEE	Knocknamona	2	2.08	432.74
14 Dec 2018 12:35	DONCASTER	Nadaitak	2	0.00	431.74
14 Dec 2018 13:10	DONCASTER	Gowiththeflow	2	0.00	430.74
14 Dec 2018 14:20	DONCASTER	Sir Mangan	2	0.00	429.74
15 Dec 2018 12:25	DONCASTER	Newtown Boy	3	1.17	428.74
15 Dec 2018 12:35	HEREFORD	Star Of Lanka	1	1.17	428.90
15 Dec 2018 13:35	DONCASTER	Rocky's Treasure	1	1.44	429.32
15 Dec 2018 15:30	HEREFORD	Logan Rocks	1	1.24	429.55
16 Dec 2018 12:20	CARLISLE	Earlofthecotswolds	1	1.15	429.69
16 Dec 2018 13:45	SOUTHWELL	Stoney Mountain	1	1.06	429.75
16 Dec 2018 15:30	CARLISLE	Rosie And Millie	2	1.19	429.93
17 Dec 2018 12:25	PLUMPTON	Collooney	2	1.13	430.05
17 Dec 2018 12:55	PLUMPTON	Ok Corral	1	1.07	430.12
17 Dec 2018 13:10	FFOS LAS	Monsieur Lecoq	1	1.22	430.33
17 Dec 2018 13:30	PLUMPTON	Mr Pumblechook	1	1.19	430.52
17 Dec 2018 18:45	WOLVERHAMPTON	Lady Lizzy	2	1.24	430.75
18 Dec 2018 12:25	SOUTHWELL (A.W)	Point Zero	1	1.21	430.94
18 Dec 2018 14:10	CATTERICK	Morraman	3	1.34	431.27
18 Dec 2018 15:00	SOUTHWELL (A.W)	Geography Teacher	1	1.33	431.58
19 Dec 2018 12:20	LUDLOW	Oakley	1	1.19	431.76
19 Dec 2018 12:30	NEWBURY	Style De Vole	2	1.17	431.93
19 Dec 2018 13:25	LUDLOW	Capeland	2	1.38	432.29
20 Dec 2018 12:30	HEXHAM	Well Above Par	2	1.17	432.45
20 Dec 2018 13:00	HEXHAM	Highland Hunter	1	1.09	432.53
20 Dec 2018 14:00	HEXHAM	Misfits	3	1.36	432.87
20 Dec 2018 14:10	EXETER	Kalahari Queen	2	1.29	433.15
20 Dec 2018 18:30	CHELMSFORD (A.W)	San Carlos	1	1.36	433.49
22 Dec 2018 12:45	NEWCASTLE	Informateur	2	1.37	433.84
22 Dec 2018 13:45	LINGFIELD (A.W)	Ghazawaat	1	1.10	433.93
22 Dec 2018 13:55	NEWCASTLE	Eternally Yours	1	1.59	434.50
22 Dec 2018 14:05	HAYDOCK	Ballymoy	1	1.31	434.79
22 Dec 2018 15:05	NEWCASTLE	Alright Sunshine	2	1.45	435.22
26 Dec 2018 12:00	WETHERBY	Mega Yeats	1	1.17	435.38

54

THE HORSE RACING PLACE BET INVESTMENT STRATEGY

Date	Course	Horse	Pos	SP	Bank
26 Dec 2018 12:15	FONTWELL	Bonza Girl	1	1.26	435.63
26 Dec 2018 12:55	WINCANTON	Posh Trish	1	1.06	435.68
26 Dec 2018 13:10	MARKET RASEN	Sir Egbert	2	1.18	435.86
26 Dec 2018 14:30	KEMPTON	Buveur D'Air	2	1.17	436.02
26 Dec 2018 16:55	WOLVERHAMPTON	Klass Action	1	1.26	436.27
27 Dec 2018 13:25	WOLVERHAMPTON	Peachey Carneha	1	1.61	436.85
27 Dec 2018 14:30	KEMPTON	Altior	1	1.08	436.93
28 Dec 2018 11:35	LINGFIELD (A.W)	Whinging Willie	2	1.15	437.06
28 Dec 2018 12:40	LINGFIELD (A.W)	Enchanting Man	2	1.37	437.41
28 Dec 2018 13:25	LEICESTER	Bright Forecast	1	1.25	437.65
28 Dec 2018 14:30	LEICESTER	Amour De Nuit	2	0.00	436.65
29 Dec 2018 11:30	SOUTHWELL (A.W)	Fenjal	2	1.29	436.92
29 Dec 2018 12:00	SOUTHWELL (A.W)	Rock Bottom	2	1.17	437.08
29 Dec 2018 12:05	NEWBURY	Song For Someor	1	1.54	437.60
29 Dec 2018 12:15	KELSO	Geronimo	1	1.39	437.96
29 Dec 2018 13:15	NEWBURY	Another Crick	1	1.64	438.58
29 Dec 2018 14:05	DONCASTER	Lady Buttons	1	1.52	439.07
29 Dec 2018 14:40	DONCASTER	Ballywood	1	1.38	439.43
30 Dec 2018 15:35	HAYDOCK	Mr Grey Sky	1	1.37	439.78
31 Dec 2018 12:10	LINGFIELD (A.W)	Gin Palace	2	1.17	439.95
01 Jan 2019 12:15	CHELTENHAM	I Can't Explain	2	1.26	440.20
01 Jan 2019 12:25	CATTERICK	Vamanos	3	1.17	439.20
01 Jan 2019 13:40	MUSSELBURGH	Forth Bridge	2	1.61	439.77
01 Jan 2019 14:10	CATTERICK	Foxtrot Juliet	3	1.15	439.91
02 Jan 2019 12:30	AYR	Johnbb	1	1.13	440.04
02 Jan 2019 13:35	AYR	Sebastopol	3	1.24	440.26
02 Jan 2019 13:55	HEREFORD	Poucor	1	1.63	440.86
02 Jan 2019 15:10	AYR	Glittering Love	1	1.38	441.22
02 Jan 2019 15:30	HEREFORD	Liberty Bella	1	1.60	441.79
02 Jan 2019 15:35	NEWCASTLE (A.W)	Sajanjl	2	1.73	442.48
02 Jan 2019 16:45	NEWCASTLE (A.W)	Kentucky Kingdo	3	1.26	442.71
03 Jan 2019 12:40	LUDLOW	Capone	1	1.11	442.82
03 Jan 2019 12:55	SOUTHWELL (A.W)	Constituent	3	1.21	443.12
03 Jan 2019 13:30	SOUTHWELL (A.W)	Francophilia	3	1.85	442.12
03 Jan 2019 16:10	CHELMSFORD (A.W)	Originaire	1	1.20	442.31
04 Jan 2019 12:45	WETHERBY	The Knot Is Tied	2	1.19	442.49
04 Jan 2019 14:20	WETHERBY	Clarendon Street	1	1.14	442.62
04 Jan 2019 14:55	WETHERBY	Nortonthorpeleg	1	1.27	442.88
04 Jan 2019 15:15	KEMPTON (A.W)	Reeth	1	1.39	443.25
04 Jan 2019 15:30	WETHERBY	Prince Llywelyn	1	1.46	443.69
04 Jan 2019 19:15	WOLVERHAMPTON	Robert L'Echelle	1	1.18	443.86
05 Jan 2019 12:15	SANDOWN	Torpillo	1	1.19	444.03
05 Jan 2019 12:40	LINGFIELD (A.W)	Forbidden Planet	1	1.27	444.29
05 Jan 2019 12:45	SANDOWN	Capeland	1	1.40	444.67
05 Jan 2019 13:35	WINCANTON	Kapcorse	1	1.11	444.77
05 Jan 2019 13:50	SANDOWN	Laurina	1	0.00	444.77
05 Jan 2019 14:15	LINGFIELD (A.W)	Straight Right	2	1.33	445.09
05 Jan 2019 15:35	SANDOWN	Monsleur Lecoq	1	2.20	446.23
06 Jan 2019 12:40	PLUMPTON	Brandon Castle	1	1.17	446.39
06 Jan 2019 13:00	NEWCASTLE (A.W)	Grey Mist	1	1.18	446.56
06 Jan 2019 13:40	PLUMPTON	Phoenix Way	1	1.30	446.85
06 Jan 2019 14:30	NEWCASTLE (A.W)	Elysees Palace	1	1.17	447.01
07 Jan 2019 12:50	MUSSELBURGH	Ontopoftheworld	1	0.00	447.01
07 Jan 2019 13:25	MUSSELBURGH	Nefyn Point	3	1.32	446.01
07 Jan 2019 15:35	MUSSELBURGH	Alright Sunshine	1	1.10	446.10
07 Jan 2019 15:50	CHEPSTOW	Cloudy Glen	1	1.27	446.35
07 Jan 2019 16:45	WOLVERHAMPTON	Blame Culture	1	1.16	446.51
08 Jan 2019 12:55	AYR	Magic Of Milan	1	1.68	447.15
08 Jan 2019 14:15	BANGOR-ON-DEE	Collooney	1	1.11	447.26
08 Jan 2019 15:25	BANGOR-ON-DEE	Two For Gold	1	1.29	447.53
08 Jan 2019 17:45	NEWCASTLE (A.W)	Set Piece	1	1.51	448.02
08 Jan 2019 18:45	NEWCASTLE (A.W)	Lorna Cole	1	1.25	448.25
09 Jan 2019 13:25	LINGFIELD (A.W)	Secret Ace	2	1.09	448.31
09 Jan 2019 13:45	TAUNTON	Khage	1	1.22	448.73
09 Jan 2019 15:15	DONCASTER	Plantagenet	2	1.63	449.33
09 Jan 2019 15:25	TAUNTON	Road To Rome	1	1.29	449.60
09 Jan 2019 15:40	TAUNTON	Global Wonder	2	1.32	449.91
10 Jan 2019 13:00	CATTERICK	Uno Mas	1	1.11	450.01
10 Jan 2019 13:45	LEICESTER	Desirable Court	1	1.10	450.10
10 Jan 2019 15:50	CATTERICK	Jimmy Rabbitte	1	1.12	450.27
10 Jan 2019 17:15	CHELMSFORD (A.W)	New King	3	1.22	450.68
11 Jan 2019 13:00	HUNTINGDON	Black Buble	1	1.38	450.84
11 Jan 2019 14:30	HUNTINGDON	Westbrook Berti	2	1.50	451.32
11 Jan 2019 15:50	SEDGEFIELD	Dares To Dream	2	1.19	451.50
11 Jan 2019 18:15	WOLVERHAMPTON	Flaming Marvel	1	1.19	451.68
12 Jan 2019 12:50	LINGFIELD (A.W)	Dashing Poet	2	1.29	451.95
12 Jan 2019 13:25	LINGFIELD (A.W)	Merhoob	2	2.06	452.96
12 Jan 2019 14:15	WETHERBY	Kauto Riko	1	1.92	451.96
12 Jan 2019 15:35	WARWICK	First Assignment	3	1.59	452.52
12 Jan 2019 17:00	NEWCASTLE (A.W)	Kareena Kapoor	1	1.35	452.66
12 Jan 2019 18:30	NEWCASTLE (A.W)	Athollblair Boy	1	1.48	453.12
13 Jan 2019 12:50	SOUTHWELL (A.W)	Eve Harrington	1	1.20	453.31
13 Jan 2019 13:00	KELSO	Lord Yeats	1	1.11	453.41
13 Jan 2019 15:40	KELSO	Achill Road Boy	1	1.48	453.86
14 Jan 2019 14:35	FFOS LAS	Whatswrongwith	1	0.00	453.86
14 Jan 2019 15:40	FFOS LAS	Quantum Of Sola	2	1.57	454.40
15 Jan 2019 13:10	LINGFIELD	Emitom	1	1.09	454.49
15 Jan 2019 13:50	NEWCASTLE	Jammin Masters	2	1.12	454.60
15 Jan 2019 14:10	LINGFIELD	Chivers	3	1.65	455.22

THE HORSE RACING PLACE BET INVESTMENT STRATEGY

Date	Course	Horse	Pos	Odds	Balance
15 Jan 2019 15:20	NEWCASTLE	Halcyon Days	2	1.86	456.04
15 Jan 2019 15:50	NEWCASTLE	Magic Of Milan	2	1.20	456.23
16 Jan 2019 13:50	LINGFIELD (A.W)	Paradise Boy	1	1.12	456.34
16 Jan 2019 14:15	NEWBURY	The Russian Doys	1	1.22	456.55
16 Jan 2019 15:00	LINGFIELD (A.W)	James Street	2	1.64	457.16
16 Jan 2019 19:30	KEMPTON (A.W)	Chica De La Noch	3	1.43	457.57
17 Jan 2019 13:45	LUDLOW	Rapper	1	1.27	457.83
17 Jan 2019 14:40	MARKET RASEN	Mrs Hyde	2	1.32	458.13
18 Jan 2019 16:45	KEMPTON (A.W)	Rock Bottom	2	1.34	458.46
19 Jan 2019 13:30	HAYDOCK	Jerrysback	2	1.61	459.04
19 Jan 2019 14:05	HAYDOCK	Mister Fisher	1	1.32	459.34
19 Jan 2019 15:10	LINGFIELD (A.W)	Probability	1	1.18	459.52
19 Jan 2019 15:25	TAUNTON	Before Midnight	1	1.20	459.71
19 Jan 2019 15:35	ASCOT	Altior	1	0.00	459.71
19 Jan 2019 15:55	TAUNTON	Railroad Junkie	2	1.31	460.00
19 Jan 2019 16:25	TAUNTON	Ellarna	3	1.37	460.36
19 Jan 2019 18:15	WOLVERHAMPTON	Your Band	3	1.24	460.58
20 Jan 2019 14:00	AYR	Destrier	1	1.15	460.73
21 Jan 2019 13:50	SEDGEFIELD	Ingleby Hollow	1	1.26	460.97
21 Jan 2019 14:20	SEDGEFIELD	Briac	1	1.43	461.38
21 Jan 2019 15:30	SEDGEFIELD	Windsor Avenue	1	1.15	461.52
21 Jan 2019 16:15	WOLVERHAMPTON	Heatherdown	1	1.48	461.98
21 Jan 2019 17:25	WOLVERHAMPTON	Kinver Edge	2	1.11	462.08
22 Jan 2019 13:10	LEICESTER	Chef D'Equipe	2	1.23	462.30
22 Jan 2019 13:40	LEICESTER	Burbank	2	0.00	461.30
22 Jan 2019 13:55	KELSO	Alizee De Janeiro	3	1.46	460.30
22 Jan 2019 15:40	LEICESTER	Forth Bridge	2	1.70	460.97
22 Jan 2019 18:45	NEWCASTLE (A.W)	Havana Rocket	1	1.25	461.21
23 Jan 2019 13:30	LINGFIELD (A.W)	Chica De La Noch	2	1.60	461.78
23 Jan 2019 14:05	LINGFIELD (A.W)	St Peters Basilica	1	1.33	462.09
25 Jan 2019 13:25	DONCASTER	Storm Goddess	1	1.10	462.19
25 Jan 2019 14:05	HUNTINGDON	Arthur's Reuben	3	1.83	462.98
25 Jan 2019 14:20	LINGFIELD (A.W)	Axel Jacklin	1	1.33	463.29
25 Jan 2019 14:40	HUNTINGDON	Magic Of Light	2	1.52	463.78
25 Jan 2019 18:15	NEWCASTLE (A.W)	Alkaamel	1	1.17	463.94
26 Jan 2019 12.40	CHELTENHAM	Adjali	3	1.28	464.2
27 Jan 2019 16.10	SEDGEFIELD	Baratineur	2	1.32	464.5
28 Jan 2019 14.05	KEMPTON	Pym	1	1.1	464.6
28 Jan 2019 17.55	WOLVERHAMPTON	Cloudlam	1	1.34	464.92
29 Jan 2019 20.15	WOLVERHAMPTON	American Grafitt	2	1.17	465.08
30 Jan 2019 20.15	WOLVERHAMPTON	Albert Finney	1	1.27	465.35
31 Jan 2019 13.35	SOUTHWELL (A.W)	Gorgeous Genera	2	1.56	465.88
31 Jan 2019 15.10	SOUTHWELL (A.W)	Scale Force	2	1.3	466.17
31 Jan 2019 19.00	NEWCASTLE (A.W)	Eve Harrington	2	1.57	466.71
31 Jan 2019 19.30	NEWCASTLE (A.W)	Lion Hearted	1	1.16	466.86
01 Feb 2019 14.50	LINGFIELD (A.W)	Water's Edge	1	1.13	466.98
01 Feb 2019 15.25	LINGFIELD (A.W)	Grey Brittain	1	1.95	467.88
01 Feb 2019 16.45	NEWCASTLE (A.W)	Creationist	1	1.16	468.04
01/02/2019 16.40	WOLVERHAMPTON	Precision Time	1	1.38	468.4
02/02/2019 12.35	LINGFIELD (A.W)	Spirit Warning	1	1.64	469.01
02/02/2019 13.45	LINGFIELD (A.W)	Kachy	1	1.24	469.24
02/02/2019 13.00	CHELMSFORD (A.W)	Orchard Star	1	1.06	469.3
04/02/2019 13.45	TAUNTON	Southfield Stone	2	1.06	469.9
04/02/2019 16.30	CHELMSFORD (A.W)	Gantier	1	1.31	470.19
04/02/2019 20.25	WOLVERHAMPTON	Marhaban	1	1.08	470.27
05/02/2019 16.30	MARKET RASEN	Loch Linnie	0	1.61	469.27
06/02/2019 14.00	AYR	Galvin	1	1.07	469.34
06/02/2019 14.10	LUDLOW	Style De Garde	2	1.38	469.7
06/02/2019 15.45	LUDLOW	Via Delle Volte	0	1.23	468.7
06/02/2019 19.15	WOLVERHAMPTON	Zorowar	1	1.3	468.99
06/02/2019 19.45	WOLVERHAMPTON	Star Of Southwol	2	1.72	469.67
13/02/2019 2.20	MUSSELBURGH	Properhinge Ging	2	1.06	469.73
13/02/2019 16.00	SOUTHWELL (A.W)	Playful Spirit	1	1.19	469.91
14/02/2019 1.25	KELSO	Dream Du Grand	1	1.06	469.97
14/02/2019 1.55	KELSO	My Old Gold	2	1.41	470.36
14/02/2019 15.35	KELSO	Aye Right	2	1.3	470.66
14/02/2019 16.00	LEICESTER	Hurricane Dylan	1	1.31	470.97
14/02/2019 20.00	CHELMSFORD (A.W)	Cirque Royal	1	1.06	471.01
15/02/2019 13.20	SANDOWN	Not Another Mus	1	1.33	471.32
15/02/2019 15.45	NEWCASTLE (A.W)	Orchid Star	1	1.04	471.36
16/02/2019 13.35	ASCOT	Top Ville Ben	0	1.97	470.36
16/02/2019 16.40	KEMPTON (A.W)	Dahawi	1	1.1	470.46
16/02/2019 19.15	KEMPTON (A.W)	Grey Brittain	0	1.32	469.46
17/02/2019 16.35	HUNTINGDON	Supakalanistic	1	1.35	468.46
17/02/2019 16.40	HUNTINGDON	Global Dominatio	0	1.35	467.46
17/02/2019 16.20	MARKET RASEN	Mixchievous	0	1.38	466.46
18/02/2019 14.00	CARLISLE	Champagne Cour	3	1.2	466.65
19/02/2019 19.00	WOLVERHAMPTON	Don't Do It	0	1.74	465.65
19/02/2019 20.00	WOLVERHAMPTON	Dawn Crusade	2	1.1	465.75
21/02/2019 17.10	HUNTINGDON	Loveherandleave	1	1.29	466.03
21/02/2019 19.10	WOLVERHAMPTON	War Tiger	1	1.29	466.31
21/02/2019 20.10	WOLVERHAMPTON	Plumette	2	1.11	466.41
21/02/2019 19.55	CHELMSFORD (A.W)	White Coat	2	1.08	466.49
22/02/2019 13.20	CATTERICK	Young Wolf	3	1.14	466.62
22/02/2019 15.05	CATTERICK	Reve	1	1.24	466.85
22/02/2019 15.35	CATTERICK	Little Bruce	0	2.2	465.85
22/02/2019 15.20	WARWICK	Uno Mas	1	1.59	466.41
22/02/2019 16.05	LINGFIELD (A.W)	Top Power	1	1.21	465.41
22/02/2019 14.40	EXETER	Epetante	1	1.12	465.52

THE HORSE RACING PLACE BET INVESTMENT STRATEGY

Date	Course	Horse	Pos	Odds	Balance
23/02/2019 14.30	CHEPSTOW	Dickie Diver	1	1.13	465.64
23/02/2019 15.05	CHEPSTOW	Jammin Masters	2	1.11	465.74
23/02/2019 15.15	LINGFIELD (A.W)	Wissahickon	1	1.14	465.87
23/02/2019 18.30	WOLVERHAMPTON	Miss Crick	1	1.38	466.23
24/02/2019 14.40	CARLISLE	Achill Road Boy	2	1.66	466.86
24/02/2019 15.10	CARLISLE	For Three	3	1.96	467.77
24/02/2019 16.15	CARLISLE	Doc Carver	2	1.38	468.13
25/02/2019 14.00	PLUMPTON	Ding Ding	1	2.11	469.18
25/02/2019 15.00	PLUMPTON	The Flying Sofa	2	1.24	469.41
25/02/2019 15.30	PLUMPTON	Brandon Castle	1	1.34	469.73
26/02/2019 15.20	CATTERICK	Louis Vac' Pouch	1	1.07	469.8
26/02/2019 15.50	CATTERICK	Shaman Du Berla	0	1.04	468.8
26/02/2019 16.50	CATTERICK	Aptly Put	2	1.68	469.45
26/02/2019 17.30	WOLVERHAMPTON	King Of Naples	1	1.3	469.74
27/02/2019 15.20	WINCANTON	Champagne Mys	2	1.13	469.86
27/02/2019 18.30	KEMPTON (A.W)	Verdana Blue	2	1.05	469.91
28/02/2019 14.35	TAUNTON	Airton	2	1.12	470.02
28/02/2019 15.10	TAUNTON	Sammylou	3	2.41	471.42
28/02/2019 15.00	LUDLOW	Earlofthecotswol	2	1.54	471.93
28/02/2019 15.35	LUDLOW	Ulan Bhute	0	1.65	470.93
28/02/2019 16.40	NEWCASTLE (A.W)	Almost Midnight	2	1.14	471.06
28/02/2019 18.15	NEWCASTLE (A.W)	Athollblair Boy	3	1.87	471.89
28/02/2019 18.30	KEMPTON (A.W)	Zaula	0	2.96	470.89
03/03/2019 14.00	HUNTINGDON	Ferrobin	1	1.09	470.98
03/03/2019 14.20	SEDGEFIELD	Arthur Mac	1	1.13	471.1
03/03/2019 15.20	SEDGEFIELD	Transpennine Sta	3	1.85	471.91

Printed in Great Britain
by Amazon